SHORT STUFF:
Ten- to Twenty-Minute Plays for Mature Actors

SHORT STUFF:
Ten- to Twenty-Minute Plays for Mature Actors

**Introduced and Compiled
by
Ann McDonough, Ph.D.**

Dramatic Publishing
Woodstock, Illinois • London, England • Melbourne, Australia

*** NOTICE ***

Professionals and amateurs are hereby warned that each play in this book is fully protected under the copyright laws of the United States of America, the British Commonwealth, including Canada, and all other countries of the Copyright Union. Plays may be used for audition purposes only without royalty; however, all plays in this volume are subject to royalty payment for: professional and amateur performances, motion pictures, lecturing, public readings, radio broadcasting, television, reprinting, and translation into foreign languages.

For royalty information and permission to perform, please refer to the permission acknowledgment pages at the end of this book to locate the source able to grant permission for public performance. The permission acknowledgment section constitutes an extension of this copyright page.

Published by The Dramatic Publishing Company
P.O. Box 129, Woodstock, IL 60098

Copyright ©MCMXCVIII by
DRAMATIC PUBLISHING

Printed in the United States of America
All Rights Reserved
(SHORT STUFF: Ten- to Twenty-Minute Plays for Mature Actors)

Cover design by Susan Carle

ISBN 0-87129-851-1

For my parents,
Dr. Anthony and Mary Del Vecchio

Illustrations: Ellis Pryce-Jones

Acknowledgments

Thank you to Julie Kunzie, who spent countless hours laying the foundation for this volume. A special thank you to Kent Brown, who lent his invaluable talents and artistic eye in the selection process, and to Gayle Sergel, whose vision in publishing works for Senior Adult Theatre is making an immense contribution in the growth and development of this ever-expanding movement.

Contents

Introduction, Ann McDonough ix

The Plays
Georgie and Sass 3
Cornbread and Beans 13
They Even Got the Rienzi 31
The Memory Club of America 43
A Man and His Plant 53
Horseshoe Bend 71
Twilight Serenade 83
Book Keeping 93
There Was a Bigness 111
Put Your Best Foot Forward 121
A Little Support 127
Ride of a Lifetime 139
Gunslinger Motel 147
Buzz 161
Paper Walls 171
Some Say Fire 181
Seen 191
Concerned Citizens 199
Starman, Wish Me Luck 207
Golden Arches 225
The Magic Bandit 239
The Sale 249

About the Playwrights 259
Permission Acknowledgments 266

Introduction

On the evening of January 5, 1997, I faced a packed ballroom in Las Vegas at the third National Senior Adult Theatre Festival kickoff. Hundreds of Senior Adult Theatre directors, playwrights, producers and actors representing forty-three companies and educational programs had come from thirty-one states and three foreign countries. When the master of ceremonies, Dr. Jeff Koep, announced that almost fourteen hundred people were attending this festival, it occurred to me with amazement and delight that Senior Adult Theatre had grown rapidly in its short history.

From humble beginnings about forty years ago, when Senior Adult Theatre encompassed primarily creative drama groups at senior citizen and community centers, this form of theatre by, for, and about older adulthood had made some major strides. In just a few short decades, the early creative drama groups had given way to oral history theatre companies. For instance, Grandparents Living Theatre in Columbus, Ohio, did not begin with a full season of plays, such as they produce today, but with oral history plays crafted by Dr. Joy Reilly with the inspiration and assistance of older citizens at senior centers.

Along with oral history presentations, other groups around the country, such as the Senior Star Showcase at Essex Community College in Baltimore, Md., and the Geritol Frolics at Great Basin College in Brainerd, Minn., were producing large-cast musical revues. Soon thereafter, at the first two National Senior Adult Theatre Festivals held by the University of Nevada, Las Vegas (UNLV), in 1993 and 1995, theatre companies and Senior Adult Theatre programs such as Indiana's Third Age Theatre from Muncie and the Senior Players of the American River Community from Sacramento were performing a variety of successful and entertaining musical and oral history revues.

Seeds of another important venue for Senior Adult Theatre, however, were also in evidence at the first festival in Las Vegas—the short play. A diverse and challenging bill of ten- fifteen- and twenty-minute plays written by UNLV Master of Fine Arts in Playwriting students was greeted with amazing enthusiasm. So successful were they that many Senior Adult Theatre practitioners across the continent have now hailed this "new" form as a dynamic, entertaining and satisfying genre of theatre for companies of older and intergenerational performers.

While this form is "new" for Senior Adult Theatre, short plays have been used for a number of years as performance and teaching pieces. These short theatrical works were used primarily in playwriting programs as exercises for playwriting students. The practice was adopted also as a means of teaching the basics of play structure and character development. In its compressed style, the short play quickly and precisely illustrates the finer points of exposition, inciting incident, growing conflict, climax and resolution.

Short Stuff playwright Jenny Laird, who is director of Prime Time Theatrics, a Senior Adult Theatre program at Northlight Theatre in Skokie, Ill., emphasizes: "As a playwright, I feel this compression is a wonderful challenge, because I must discover all the ways this one, small, dramatized moment allows me to show my characters as the complete and whole beings that they are."

The challenge for the performers is considerable, as well, for the actor in the short play has the same responsibility as his/her colleague in a longer work. In fact, it would be a mistake for the actor to think that s/he has to do less work because the play is shorter. The truth of the matter is that the actor's work is highly compressed and intensified. The actor must have a fully developed characterization from the moment the curtain goes up. If not, the play will end before the actor has fully communicated what she/he needs and wants.

Playwright Mark Jensen, who contributed *Buzz* and *The Magic Bandit*, elaborates upon the actor's task by emphasizing that "actors and directors will find they will have to create as much background on the characters as they would in a long piece. Perhaps they might even discover there is more subtext to fill in as there is less material to explore. Keep in mind that the short play is not a 'lesser' form; it's a 'different' form."

It is this very quality—the condensed nature of short plays—that pleased my older students in UNLV's Senior Adult Theatre program. They greeted this genre, when I first introduced it, with surprise and delight. They had not considered before that a short play could be so successful and satisfying from the standpoint of the audience as well as the performer. Several older students were eager to participate, especially because of the reduced demands the short form placed upon increasing health difficulties and their busy schedules.

Many older adults face health problems that may make lengthy memorization very difficult. In addition, older adults are increasingly helping to raise grandchildren, as well as going back to work for economic reasons. Thus, senior adults today often cope with complicated schedules, and a shorter rehearsal period with less memorization seems to be more manageable.

Another useful feature of the short play is that bills of these works may be organized around a particular theme, or a company may use these short dramatic pieces along with the presentation of a longer one-act play, or along with a series of monologues. In addition, with typically no more than two to four characters in each play, the settings tend to be simple. Thus, when presenting selections from *Short Stuff*, a Senior Adult Theatre company or program has the flexibility of using a small company of actors to play all the roles in all of the plays, or casting a large number of actors who would each play a single role in one of the pieces.

Producing companies also will enjoy the distinct economic advantage of being able to use one flexible set for most of the plays in this volume. Set pieces can simply be arranged as needed, depending upon the unique requirements of a particular play. For instance, a table and four or five chairs in varying configurations can be used for *Golden Arches*, *Book Keeping*, *Georgie and Sass*, *A Little Support*, *Cornbread and Beans* and *Seen*, among others. Besides being cost-effective and flexible, using the same basic set for all of the pieces will provide a visual unity which helps to tie the various plays together. Furthermore, a simple, singular set, such as a table and chairs, makes touring these plays a very manageable proposition.

Indeed, audiences in a variety of venues, from nursing homes to grade schools to the local community theatre, will enjoy the parade of plots and characters in this volume, because they feature older adults in situations that are reflective of aging today. Doug Hill's *Seen*, for instance, is a ten-minute play that examines a rapidly growing phenomenon—older adults returning to college. *A Little Support*, by L.B. Hamilton, is the story of two older sisters who are processing past issues in their relationship; David Alex's *Ride of a Lifetime* features a wife who "still has plenty of spunk left in her" and a husband who "still has a twinkle in his eye"; and Kent Brown's *Put Your Best Foot Forward* presents a cleaning lady who rediscovers her sense of personal beauty. The pieces in this volume are crafted with a sensitivity to today's seniors who are alive and vibrant and struggling to live, instead of falling into the "rocking chair" syndrome.

When I next face an opening-night audience at future National Senior Adult Theatre festivals, I hope to acknowledge several exciting developments: increasing numbers of Senior Adult Theatre actors, directors and playwrights, and many more companies performing bills of short plays that reflect the excitement, drama, sadness, adventure and humor of older adulthood. To that end, *Short Stuff* is intended to make a small contribution. In this volume, we have presented a range of mature characters striving to live with dignity and humor as they set about to resolve many of life's most enduring questions. Within these characters' struggles, there can be found inspiration as well as laughter for a wide variety of audiences, and tremendous artistic opportunities for young and old alike.

THE PLAYS

GEORGIE AND SASS
by
Jenny Laird

CHARACTERS

SASS: A thin woman in her late-60s.

GEORGIE: Sass' roommate, also in her late-60s.

PLACE: Sass and Georgie's kitchen.

TIME: The present. Early morning.

GEORGIE AND SASS

SETTING: *A somewhat large kitchen but not very modern. The appliances are about twenty years old but very clean. There is a breakfast table against a wall which is cluttered with kitchen stuff: salt and pepper, honey bear, sugar, etc.*

AT RISE: *Lights up on SASS sitting at the kitchen table reading a book. She is in her robe, a turban-type scarf tied around her head. GEORGIE enters dressed like a breath of fresh air. She is full of energy this morning, and is on her way out.*

SASS. You're up early this mornin'.
GEORGIE. You snooze you lose.
SASS. Lose what?
GEORGIE. What're you makin'?
SASS. Poached...per usual. *(GEORGIE pours herself some orange juice.)*
GEORGIE. You know, when I was a kid my brother Timmy told me the yellow part was the chicken's brain. I've never liked eggs since.
SASS. Where are you off to today?
GEORGIE. I don't see how people eat anything in the morning. *(GEORGIE guzzles the orange juice.)*
SASS. I thought having a roommate meant sharing a room.

GEORGIE. Are you gonna be around this afternoon?
SASS. One can only hope. *(Silence.)* Why do all of your questions sound like requests...orders?
GEORGIE. IT WAS A QUESTION. In my head it had one of those curly things at the end of it.
SASS. I saw a hummingbird this morning. I haven't even put the feeder out yet.
GEORGIE. Because a man's coming by...
SASS. A man?
GEORGIE. The kitchen floor man.
SASS. Mr. Clean. Mr. Tidy Bowl. Except for Brawny, I get them all confused.
GEORGIE. I'm thinking of redoing the floor.
SASS. Is my water boiling?
GEORGIE. No. *(Pause.)* What, you don't think it needs new tile?
SASS. Tile! This isn't tile...this is vinyl...something or other. I've had this particular floor for twenty years, it's easy to clean. I like easy-to-clean.
GEORGIE. Well I just thought—
SASS. What do we need tile for?
GEORGIE. I don't know...it feels cool in the summer?
SASS. First day of spring and you're already to summer. Besides, tile is hard to clean, AND it's noisy.
GEORGIE. Black and white checkers...like you see in the *Better Homes and Gardens* kitchens. And maybe a bay window...here, by the breakfast table. You could see your birds without ever leaving your chair!
SASS. You should save that money.

GEORGIE. I don't wanna save that money! I wanna spend! Spend! I have it and I want to spend it.
SASS. Well "spend spend" it on something other than a kitchen floor. I like my floor just the way it is.
GEORGIE. There's something wonderful about the thought of spending Joe's hard-earned money on something as frivolous as a black and white kitchen floor!
SASS. You might be a little more appreciative...he didn't have to leave you that money—
GEORGIE. Malarkey! *(Imitating.)* "He didn't have to leave you that money"... I slept with The Callous for thirty years, didn't I? I figured it out with a calculator, last night, after taxes, I made about two dollars a night. Honey, Cary Grant couldn't have found it that cheap. *(GEORGIE grabs her purse.)*
SASS. Where are you going?
GEORGIE. I told you, to the lamp store.
SASS. No, you didn't tell me.
GEORGIE. Well I'm telling you now.
SASS. Aren't you going to ask if you can pick anything up for me? *(GEORGIE spots a bird out the window.)*
GEORGIE. Oh look, there's a cardinal!
SASS. No wonder you never got along with Joe...
GEORGIE *(quietly)*. They're such regal birds.
SASS. A Marx Brothers movie. *(GEORGIE, scared, turns around and stares at SASS.)*
GEORGIE. Pardon me?
SASS. That's what you can pick up for me while you're out gallivanting around town. I don't spend the entire day watching birds, you know.

GEORGIE. Sass...no. *(SASS shows her the cover of Norman Cousin's book* Anatomy of an Illness as Perceived by the Patient.*)*
SASS. Says here...anyone...it doesn't matter, as long as it makes you laugh.
GEORGIE. Where'd you find that book?
SASS. Joe left it to me. Pretty thoughtful for The Callous, wouldn't you say?
GEORGIE. Yes, "left" it to you because he died, Sass. Died trying to laugh himself well. I'll tell you who's laughing, Missy, that...that "doctor." He's laughing all the way to the bank.
SASS. I wanna try it, Georgie.
GEORGIE. Jesus H. Christ, Joe's living proof...dying proof, that it doesn't work!
SASS. I'm tired of poached eggs and dry toast. I want food. I want my hair back. I want to go to the lamp store. I want to laugh, goddamn it, I mean REALLY laugh.
GEORGIE. The Marx Brothers aren't even funny. I'm funny. I'll make you laugh. I'll drive you to your treatments naked. That oughta be good for something. Please. Sass. Joe was a crazy old loon.
SASS. I'm tired, Georgie.
GEORGIE. Ugggh! These New-Age "holistic" doctors. Those people were burned at the stake not too long ago, and for good reason.
SASS. It's worth a try.
GEORGIE. See! That's exactly what they rely on! It's worth a try to play the lottery too, but you don't give up your entire social security check to do so, do you? No.

SASS. I'd give it up if the government were bankrupt.
GEORGIE. What're you tryin' to say...? You can't afford the chemo? Is that it?
SASS. No.
GEORGIE. Because I just happen to have Joe's big fat check comin' my way, our way—
SASS. I'm saying...the chemo isn't working.
GEORGIE *(pause).* Your water's boiling. *(GEORGIE breaks an egg to poach.)*
SASS. Don't, I can get that. *(SASS gets out of her chair and moves to the stove. GEORGIE breaks another egg into the pot.)* I said I can do it myself.
GEORGIE. The least I can do is poach you an egg. Believe it or not, I know how to do a few things!
SASS. Give me that. *(SASS and GEORGIE struggle for the pot.)*
GEORGIE. Sit down, Sass.
SASS. You're gonna hurt yourself.
GEORGIE. Let go of me! *(The pot, water and eggs spill to the floor. SASS immediately begins cleaning the floor.)*
SASS. See!
GEORGIE. Let me do that. *(GEORGIE tries to help.)*
SASS. You've done enough. *(SASS pushes her away.)*
GEORGIE. Let me help you.
SASS. Go buy your lamp.
GEORGIE *(hurt).* Sass, I— *(SASS picks up the pot. A chunk of the vinyl floor is burned onto the bottom of the pot.)*
SASS. I guess you'll get your new floor, after all.
GEORGIE. I don't care about the floor.

SASS. Yes, you do. That's all you care about.
GEORGIE. I just wanted to make this place...brighter... for you. For us. *(SASS does not respond.)* I was trying to help. *(Still no response.)* What do you want me to say? I'm sorry I'm well. Is that it? You should be glad one of us is well to take care of the other. *(Still no response as SASS continues cleaning. GEORGIE grabs an egg and drops it on the floor in front of SASS. SASS does not look up but continues to clean.)* You're more stubborn than denture stains. *(GEORGIE drops another egg. Still no response from SASS other than her continual sponging.)* There goes another chicken's brain. *(Dropping another egg.)* Hey, Ma, look, no hands! It's magic, now you see it... *(Dropping another egg.)* Now you don't. *(The egg falls on SASS' head.)* Uh oh. *(SASS finally looks up, as if she's somewhere in between laughing and crying.)*
SASS. You wench. *(She stands and cracks an egg on GEORGIE's head.)* I heard protein's good for the hair. *(GEORGIE, laughing, cracks another egg on SASS' head.)*
GEORGIE. Makes it shiny and bright!
SASS. I don't like bright. *(SASS, laughing, reaches for another egg and cracks it on GEORGIE.)* I never have. *(Both are laughing together now.)*
GEORGIE. Oh, yeah! *(GEORGIE reaches for another egg.)*
SASS. Yeah.
GEORGIE. Damn.
SASS. What?

GEORGIE. I'm out of ammunition. *(They're both cracking up now at the sight of each other.)* Come here, you. *(GEORGIE grabs a clean sponge and begins cleaning SASS' head, which is still covered with the turban-scarf.)*

SASS. I've never liked bright, Georgie. It's just the way I am. I loved 1973 when Tom let me redecorate... I bought brown corduroy couches and dark green shags and mustard-yellow lamps and this brown vinyl floor. Real earth tones. I think I must have been a cave woman at one time—

GEORGIE. Did you read THAT in Joe's book too?

SASS. No. I just like the thought of it. More than one life. More than one chance... don't you?

GEORGIE. Hell no! Once is enough for me.

SASS. I don't want to die. Not yet anyway. Not while I'm alive. Here, give me that. *(SASS rinses the sponge and cleans GEORGIE's hair.)*

GEORGIE. Knowing my luck, I'd get a second life but end up married to another Joe Callous Mcphereson.

SASS. He wasn't so bad.

GEORGIE. How did we ever become friends?

SASS. Friends, who said we were friends?

GEORGIE. I'll tell ya, one thing he was good at, was takin' care of his pine cone when she was sick. All I had to do was cry "flu" and he'd have me tucked beneath ten wool blankets, surrounded by hot broth and Ovaltine. He'd find something funny on the tube, and then he'd curl up next to me and hold me tight like he was keeping me from falling into some big carnivorous crater.

SASS. That sounds nice.
GEORGIE. It was.
SASS. And, Georgie, the Marx Brothers ARE funny.
GEORGIE. I know. Not as funny as me driving naked. But tucked under enough blankets, and with the right person, I suppose they'll do.
SASS. Maybe that's what Joe was missing in his therapy...someone to—
GEORGIE. Maybe.
SASS. It's worth a try. *(GEORGIE holds SASS' hand.)*
GEORGIE. Yes, it is. It certainly is. *(Lights fade to black.)*

END

CORNBREAD AND BEANS
by
Earl Reimer

CHARACTERS

ALICE: A waitress with a romantic outlook on life.

HOWARD: 72, a crusty old bachelor, set in his ways.

ELLIE: 65, not set in her ways. Faces life on her terms, which may change.

PLACE: A restaurant.

TIME: Early evening.

CORNBREAD AND BEANS

AT RISE: *HOWARD is seated in the restaurant, waiting impatiently for someone to arrive. ALICE pauses at the table.*

ALICE. Your other party hasn't come yet?
HOWARD. No, she hasn't!
ALICE. What time were you expecting her?
HOWARD. Seven o'clock! She said she'd be here at seven!
ALICE. Well, that's only twenty minutes. You have to give us ladies the option of being a bit late once in a while, you know.
HOWARD. I'm never late!
ALICE. I see. Would you like some more coffee?
HOWARD. No!
ALICE. Well, I'll bring her over as soon as she gets here.
HOWARD. OK.
ALICE. How will I recognize her?
HOWARD. I don't know!
ALICE. I beg your pardon?
HOWARD. I don't know!
ALICE. You don't?
HOWARD. No. I've never met her!
ALICE. You haven't?
HOWARD. No!

ALICE. I see! *(A slight pause.)* Oh, is this one of those Date-a-Mate things, or something like that?

HOWARD. Well, maybe.

ALICE. Well, isn't that sweet? So there's a little fire left in the old stove yet, huh?

HOWARD. There won't be if she doesn't get here pretty soon.

ALICE. Well, I'm sure she will. Do you know her name?

HOWARD. Uh, it's Helen, I think.

ALICE. Helen. That's a nice name. Well, I'll bring her to your table as soon as she gets here.

HOWARD. OK.

(ALICE smiles, then exits. HOWARD takes another sip of his coffee, looks at his watch, then drums impatiently on the table while glancing at the door. He then reaches into his pocket, pulls out a sheet of paper as if to confirm the date and time, nods his head emphatically that he is right and puts the paper back in his pocket. He takes another sip of his coffee, glances at his watch again, and starts drumming on the table as ALICE returns with ELLIE who is very self-assured and not at all apologetic about being late.)

ALICE. Here he is.

ELLIE. Thanks.

ALICE. Now, you two have fun! Toodle-ooo! *(She waves coyly at them as she exits. ELLIE takes off her coat and puts it on the seat on her side of the booth.)*

ELLIE. Hi, I'm Ellie. Are you Harold?

HOWARD. Howard!
ELLIE. Howard, that's right.
HOWARD. You're late!
ELLIE. Well, I just couldn't get away from my neighbor, and then when I finally did, I was held up by two trains.
HOWARD. Hm-mph! *(ELLIE sits down.)*
ELLIE. So. Have you ordered yet?
HOWARD. NO. I waited for you!
ELLIE. Oh. Well, that was nice of you, Henry.
HOWARD. It's Howard! Twenty-five minutes!
ELLIE. What?
HOWARD. I've waited twenty-five minutes.
ELLIE. Well, good for you. We'll send you a sucker and a deputy sheriff's badge.
HOWARD. What?
ELLIE. Oh, nothing. Just a little joke. So you haven't ordered?
HOWARD. No!
ELLIE. Why not?
HOWARD. I said I waited for you.
ELLIE. That's right. You did. *(She picks up a menu.)* Do you know what you're going to have?
HOWARD. Of course. Meat loaf and broccoli.
ELLIE. What do you mean, "of course"?
HOWARD. It's Thursday!
ELLIE. So?
HOWARD. I always eat meat loaf and broccoli on Thursday.
ELLIE. Always?
HOWARD. Always!

ELLIE. Well, that's a little weird.
HOWARD. I don't think so.
ELLIE. Well, whatever rattles your chain.
HOWARD. What?
ELLIE. Don't worry about it, Hubert.
HOWARD. Howard! My name is Howard!!
ELLIE. Good for you! I like people who are proud of their name!

(ALICE returns.)

ALICE. All ready to order?
HOWARD. Yes. I'll have meat loaf and broccoli.
ALICE. All right. Anything to drink?
HOWARD. Just coffee.
ALICE. Sugar?
HOWARD. Black.
ALICE. Very good. And what about you, ma'am?
ELLIE. Well, I'm not very hungry. I think I'll just have a piece of apple pie.
HOWARD. Pie?
ELLIE. Apple.
ALICE. Very good. Anything to drink?
ELLIE. Just coffee.
ALICE. Black?
ELLIE. No. Cream and sugar.
ALICE. All right. Well, you two just sit back and enjoy yourselves. Just have fun, fun, fun! *(She exits.)*
HOWARD. What a busybody!
ELLIE. Oh, she's all right.

HOWARD. I'm glad you think so.

ELLIE. So, tell me. Where do you live, and what...why are you staring at me that way, Hughie?

HOWARD. For the tenth time it's not Hughie and it's not Hubert, it's Harold!

ELLIE. Oh, really. I thought...

HOWARD. I mean Howard. H-O-W-A-R-D! Howard. You got that?

ELLIE. My, we're a little touchy today, aren't we, Howie? *(HOWARD starts to bristle again.)*

HOWARD. Not Howie...

ELLIE. Oh, we don't even do abbreviations, huh? All right, but you still haven't answered my question. Why were you staring at me like that?

HOWARD. You must have had a hard life!

ELLIE. Well, I have, but so what?

HOWARD. Well, you don't look like you're under sixty.

ELLIE. I'm not. I'm sixty-five.

HOWARD. But I distinctly asked the agency for someone under sixty.

ELLIE. Oh, yes, they did mention that. So I fudged a little.

HOWARD. But that's misrepresentation! That's not being...

ELLIE. Oh, chill out, Howard. You're not exactly a stand-in for Robert Redford, you know. It said you were seventy-two.

HOWARD. Well, yes but... I mean...

ELLIE. It's no big deal. So you're seven years older than I am instead of twelve. So what! You're not going to get a Playboy bunny at your age, anyway.

HOWARD. Yes, I know, but the fact is...

(ALICE returns with the food, interrupting the conversation.)

ALICE. Here we are. Meat loaf and...broccoli. Here's your pie, ma'am. Oh, yes, sir, and here's the coleslaw that goes with it.
HOWARD. Coleslaw?
ALICE. You don't want it?
HOWARD. Can I have a dinner salad instead?
ALICE. I'm afraid there aren't any substitutions with the special, sir. But I can bring you a dinner salad for ninety-five cents extra.
HOWARD. Ninety-five cents? Why should I have to pay ninety...
ELLIE. Aw, go ahead and splurge, Howard. You're only seventy-two once!
HOWARD. I know that— But I don't see why I...
ELLIE *(to ALICE)*. Oh, go ahead and bring him a dinner salad. I'll pay for it.
ALICE. All right. What kind of dressing?
ELLIE. Thousand island.
HOWARD. French!
ELLIE. French it is.
ALICE. Got it! *(She exits.)*
HOWARD. I can pay for it. That's not the point! The point is...
ELLIE. It's a gift, Howard, from me to you. It's not polite to complain about gifts.

HOWARD. But...

ELLIE. So just shut up and eat your mush!

HOWARD. What?

ELLIE. It's just a joke, Howard. I say that to all my friends.

HOWARD. Hhmph! *(He holds up the coleslaw.)* But what about this? *(ELLIE takes it.)*

ELLIE. Here, give it to me. I'll eat it!

HOWARD. You'll eat it?

ELLIE. It's Thursday, isn't it? I always have coleslaw and pie on Thursdays.

HOWARD *(suspiciously)*. Are you making fun of me, Helen?

ELLIE. It's Ellie.

HOWARD. What?

ELLIE. My name is Ellie.

HOWARD. Ellie?

ELLIE. Yes.

HOWARD. But the sheet I got from Have-a-Friend said your name was Helen.

ELLIE. Oh, it is, officially, I guess. But everyone calls me Ellie.

HOWARD. How do you get Ellie out of Helen?

ELLIE. Easy. You just drop the "h" off the front and the "n" off the back. No "h," no "n," you get Ellie.

HOWARD. Well, I think that's very strange.

ELLIE. Well, it probably is. So let's talk about something else. So what do you like to do?

HOWARD. I like to fish.

ELLIE. Yes, I saw that in your ad. What else?

HOWARD. What?

ELLIE. What else do you do besides fish?

HOWARD. Not much.

ELLIE. Well, you don't fish every day, do you, Howard?

HOWARD. Almost every day.

ELLIE. That's unnatural!

HOWARD. I don't think so!

ELLIE. Do you like to travel?

HOWARD. Well, I go to different lakes.

ELLIE. To sail?

HOWARD. No, to fish.

ELLIE. Of course. How silly of me. Do you play any games?

HOWARD. Games?

ELLIE. Yes.

HOWARD. Like what?

ELLIE. Oh, like euchre or rummy?

HOWARD. Nope. Don't like card games!

ELLIE. How about Yahtzee?

HOWARD. Nope. Don't like dice games!

ELLIE. Monopoly?

HOWARD. Don't like the little green houses!

ELLIE. What's the matter with them?

HOWARD. I keep landing on them. They take all my money.

ELLIE. I see! Do you play checkers? Or don't you like to put round counters on square spaces?

HOWARD. I know the moves. I play once in a while.

ELLIE. Ever go to concerts, Howard?

HOWARD. Yeah, I like music some. We used to go to the symphony once in a while.

ELLIE. How about plays?

HOWARD. Yeah. Like dinner theatre. I like that.

ELLIE. Good. I'm glad you're not a total fishbrain, Howard. Are you widowed or divorced?

HOWARD. What?

ELLIE. I asked if you were widowed or divorced?

HOWARD. You're not supposed to ask me that.

ELLIE. Who says?

HOWARD. Well, Have-a-Friend. It says right on the front page of the manual that you're not supposed to talk about your past at all, and especially about your marital status. Didn't you see that?

ELLIE. Of course I did. But what do they know? What are you supposed to do? Forget you were hooked up with the wrong jerk for twenty-six years? That's silly!

HOWARD. Well, but it says that...

ELLIE. It can't be done, Howard! So don't worry about it! So, are you widowed or divorced?

HOWARD. Well, I...I...I'm a widower.

ELLIE. Widowed, huh? That's a surprise.

HOWARD. Why?

ELLIE. She must have been a saint!

HOWARD. Why do you say that?

ELLIE. I read your ad, remember?

HOWARD. So what does that...

(ALICE returns with HOWARD's salad.)

ALICE. Here you are, sir. A dinner salad with French dressing. Now you enjoy.

HOWARD. OK.
ALICE. If there's anything else you need, just let me know.
HOWARD. OK.
ALICE. If you need cake, candles or champagne, just call for Alice.
ELLIE. All right!
ALICE. Remember, fun, fun, fun! *(She leaves.)*
HOWARD. Boy, is she strange!
ELLIE. She's got a good heart!
HOWARD. I think she's just an airbrain.
ELLIE. Oh, eat your broccoli!
HOWARD. So what did you mean?
ELLIE. About what?
HOWARD. About my ad. You said my wife was probably a saint.
ELLIE. And was she?
HOWARD. Well, yes, I guess.
ELLIE. I thought so.
HOWARD. Why? *(ELLIE takes a small mirror out of her purse and hands it to HOWARD.)*
ELLIE. Here, hold this for me, will you?
HOWARD. What?
ELLIE. I want you to hold the mirror for me so I can touch up my makeup. *(She starts applying lipstick.)*
HOWARD. Now?
ELLIE. Yes.
HOWARD. Here?
ELLIE. I've had a very busy day, Herman.
HOWARD. Howard!
ELLIE. Higher.

HOWARD. No, Howard!
ELLIE. I mean the mirror! Higher!
HOWARD. Oh!
ELLIE. That's good.
HOWARD. This is embarrassing!
ELLIE. Nonsense. People will just think you're a devoted husband.
HOWARD. No, they won't. They'll think that...

(ALICE returns.)

ALICE. Now, is there anything else that... *(She sees HOWARD holding the mirror.)* Oh! Now, isn't that sweet!
HOWARD. Oh, brother!
ALICE. That is so cute! *(She bends over to look into the mirror.)* Do you mind if I check my makeup, too?
HOWARD. Oh!
ALICE. Hold still now! There. Very good. *(She fluffs her hair. She pats HOWARD on the shoulder.)* That is so sweet! So, is there anything I can get anyone?
HOWARD. A bigger mirror!
ALICE. You're funny! Well, here's your bill. If you want anything more, just call. *(She exits.)*
HOWARD. So why do you think she was?
ELLIE. Why do I think who was what?
HOWARD. What we were talking about. Why do you think my wife was a saint?
ELLIE. I said that?
HOWARD. Yes, you did. You said you could tell that from my ad.

ELLIE. That's right. I did.

HOWARD. Why?

ELLIE. How many people have answered your ad, Howard?

HOWARD. Well...

ELLIE. If you count me and get two more, you'll have three, right?

HOWARD. Well, yes.

ELLIE. Do you expect to hear from any more ladies?

HOWARD. Well, yes.

ELLIE. Well, I wouldn't hold my breath, Howard.

HOWARD. Why?

ELLIE. You might turn blue first.

HOWARD. Why do you say that?

ELLIE. Did you read your ad, Howard?

HOWARD. Yeah. What's the matter with it?

ELLIE. Well, when you start out with "On Monday I eat cornbread and beans, on Tuesday I eat liver and onions, on Wednesday I eat pork chops," that's not really a big romantic come-on, Howard.

HOWARD. Well, the Have-a-Friend people said to list what you like.

ELLIE. They weren't asking for a menu, Howard.

HOWARD. I know, but I thought...

ELLIE. Don't you think that's a little demanding?

HOWARD. Why?

ELLIE. Well, suppose I invited you over for dinner on Monday. Now, I'm not doing that, mind you, but if I did would you expect me to fix you something special, or would you eat what I gave you?

HOWARD. Monday? Well, that's when I usually eat cornbread and beans.
ELLIE. Wrong, Howard.
HOWARD. Wrong?
ELLIE. Not in my house you don't!
HOWARD. Why? What would you serve?
ELLIE. Oh, I don't know. Maybe spaghetti!
HOWARD. Spaghetti?? On Monday night?
ELLIE. Why not?
HOWARD. No beans?
ELLIE. Not a one.
HOWARD. Why not?
ELLIE. It's simple, Howard. "Beans, beans, the magical fruit, the more you eat the more you toot." Any more questions?
HOWARD. Well, that's... that's embarrassing to talk about that.
ELLIE. Well, it's a lot better to talk about it than it is to...
HOWARD. All right, I understand!
ELLIE. And then what if I told you I don't like to fish?
HOWARD. You don't?
ELLIE. What if I said I'd sooner watch paint dry. That I'd rather go bowling!
HOWARD. Bowling?
ELLIE. Yes. Did you ever try it, Howard?
HOWARD. No, but I don't see how...
ELLIE. If you haven't tried it, don't knock it, Howard!
HOWARD. Well! *(There is a pause.)*
ELLIE. Well, I guess this didn't work out too good, did it?
HOWARD. I guess not!

ELLIE. I don't like what you eat or what you do, and you don't like what I eat or what I do.

HOWARD. I guess not!

ELLIE. So I guess we'd better look for someone else!

HOWARD. I guess so!

ELLIE. Well, good. *(She rises and starts to put her coat on.)* I guess I'll be going, then. *(She turns to go.)*

HOWARD. Can I ask you just one question?

ELLIE. What?

HOWARD. Just why did you answer my ad, anyway?

ELLIE. I don't know!

HOWARD. You don't know?

ELLIE. Well...

HOWARD. You can do better than that. You've got an answer for everything else!

ELLIE. Well, actually, I like to fish, too.

HOWARD. But you said you'd sooner watch paint dry!

ELLIE. No, I didn't.

HOWARD. You did, too. I heard you!

ELLIE. No, I didn't. I said, what *if* I told you I'd rather watch paint dry.

HOWARD. Well, it's the same thing, isn't it?

ELLIE. No, it isn't. That's a big *if*. I was testing you, Howard!

HOWARD. Well?

ELLIE. You flunked!

HOWARD. Well, I don't think it's fair. If you like to fish you should have told me.

ELLIE. Why?

HOWARD. It might have made a difference.

ELLIE. How?

HOWARD. Well, I'd'a told you about some good places to fish, and how my father used to take me with him and...

ELLIE. Your father taught you how to fish?

HOWARD. Sure did.

ELLIE. So did mine!

HOWARD. He did?

ELLIE. We went every Saturday morning just as the sun came up, while it was still cool.

HOWARD. Yeah? We did, too. That way we'd get the best spot.

ELLIE. Right!

HOWARD. We'd fish for three hours every Saturday morning.

ELLIE. So would we!

HOWARD *(with nostalgia)*. Those were great days.

ELLIE *(also remembers)*. Yeah!

HOWARD *(coming back to the present)*. Well!

ELLIE *(does, too)*. Yeah! *(She starts to leave.)*

HOWARD. So! Do you want to sit down and talk a bit?

ELLIE. No, I think I better get going.

HOWARD. Well, OK. *(She starts to leave, then turns back.)*

ELLIE. So do you want to come over for dinner Monday night or not?

HOWARD. Monday night? Well, sure, that'll be all right. What time?

ELLIE. I eat at six, sharp.

HOWARD. OK.

ELLIE. I live at 2820 Riverview.

HOWARD. OK.

ELLIE *(starts to leave, then turns back)*. It won't be nothing special.

HOWARD. That's OK.

ELLIE. Probably spaghetti.

HOWARD. Spaghetti.

ELLIE. Right. *(She starts to leave.)* No beans, Howard.

HOWARD. All right, no beans. *(She starts to leave again, then once again turns back.)*

ELLIE. Maybe cornbread!

HOWARD. Oh. OK. *(ELLIE exits. HOWARD watches her go, then turns back.)* Cornbread and spaghetti? *(He contemplates this a bit, then shrugs.)* Well...maybe! *(Curtain.)*

END

THEY EVEN GOT THE RIENZI
by
Claudia Allen

CHARACTERS

MR. PONAZECKI: an elderly citizen of Chicago.

A male and a female to interject.

PLACE: The city of Chicago.

TIME: 1980s.

THEY EVEN GOT THE RIENZI was first presented at The Great Chicago Playwrights Exposition which was produced by Victory Gardens Theater and the Body Politic Theatre in 1987.

For Studs Terkel

THEY EVEN GOT THE RIENZI

AT RISE: *MR. PONAZECKI is wearing an oversized, wornout-looking robe that once fit. He is leaning on a walker. He is an infirm, saddened old man with still some spark of life, of humor. [The actor and the director should use their own judgment as to how much he should move—or not.] He's just telling his story, though every so often a voice—or possibly an actor—will enter in for a brief flashback effect.*

MR. PONAZECKI. I went into the hospital last year for surgery on my left lung. Now—no left lung. I know nobody thought I was gonna make it, 'cause they put me in this room where people kept dyin'. I mean they was droppin' like flies. Not the kinda place where you'd wanna get too fond'a anybody. Not unless you was plannin' to join 'em in the morgue, an' I wasn't. Not right away anyway. Despite expectations to the contrary—I mean that hospital practically had my hole dug—I wasn't ready to go. When the nurses checked me in the morning I know they was always surprised to see me still breathin'.

FEMALE VOICE. Whatdayamean there's a pulse? Oh, there is not. Look at him... You swear you feel a pulse? Give me that wrist.

MR. PONAZECKI. They'd lean right down in my face 'n stare. One day I winked at one of 'em; scared the shit out of her. This went on for four, five days till they finally musta give up on the idea I was gonna croak any minute, 'cause they moved me into a nicer room not so close to the morgue. It even had a viewa the lake. The boys from the Rienzi come to visit me once, an' they said it looked to them like I was a king livin' in splendor.

MALE VOICE. Will you look at this. This sonofabitch is livin' just like a king. No wonder he don't wanna leave.

MR. PONAZECKI. But I did wanna leave. You don't know. Jesus, I wanted to go home with 'em to that ole Rienzi Hotel somethin' awful. But I had to wait; had to build up my strength. Only havin' one lung left me without as much wind as I was used to, so I had to stay in the hospital an' eat spinach like Popeye. Exercise. Don't get me wrong. I'm not complainin'. One lung's plenty unless you wanna jog to Milwaukee or be a mud wrestler or somethin'. I got so I could cripple my way around the hospital pretty good, but I didn't go far. It's such a big place I got lost a coupla times, an' that was embarrassing. People either patronize you 'cause you're old or they get irritated—same reason.

FEMALE VOICE. Well, where is your room? Don't you know where your room is?

MR. PONAZECKI. Fall came— I watched it out my window—an' I wished I was sittin' over by the Elk Memorial on Diversey, shootin' the breeze with the boys, watchin' the trees in Lincoln Park turn color; sittin' there in the cold till our false teeth almost chattered outta our heads. Watchin' the colors turn out a hospital window just don't compare. I got to feelin' real lonely. Nobody'd come to see me in a long time. Some of my pals at the Rienzi were kinda on the senile side; maybe they'd forgot I was still alive. I watched the TV some but not much 'cause I'd seen all the shows. Well, maybe not them exact shows, but I been watchin' TV for thirty years; nothin's new. I miss Ed Sullivan an' Imogene Coca. An' live TV. Remember that? They used to do live TV right here in Chicago, right over at Channel 5. Dave Garroway, Studs Terkel, guys like that. TV's so slick now, it's boring. But I watch it sometimes, when it's all there is.

FEMALE VOICE. I can't let you go. I just can't!

MALE VOICE. You don't have a choice, Monica. Grace didn't die in that plane crash.

FEMALE VOICE. No!

MALE VOICE. Which means...

MR. PONAZECKI *(switches off imaginary TV)*. He's married to both of 'em. Next thing you know he'll have amnesia. Same old stuff. I liked night 'cause nobody was pokin' needles in me an' I could lay there in peace an' pretend I was back at my sandblaster. That's what I did way back when, run a sandblaster. I blasted all them snobby houses on the Gold Coast in my day. After I got too old, my lungs half-shot, I janitored at the Century movie theater on Clark Street right up to when they gutted the old place an' put in a shopping mall with a buncha fancy stores an' a glass elevator.

FEMALE VOICE. Isn't this just the cutest dress?

MALE VOICE. Oh, it's you.

MR. PONAZECKI. I'd give my eye teeth—if I still had 'em—to see the Century back the way it used to be. It was a pleasure to clean. When you went to a movie in one of them old Chicago picture palaces, you really knew you were steppin' out on the town. Class with a capital C. But them days are over. The past five years or so I been livin' in retirement. Watchin' my suits get too big for me an' livin' at the Rienzi Hotel. I know it don't sound very exciting, not like runnin' a sandblaster or cleanin' up after Doris Day 'n Clark Gable, but livin' at the ole Rienzi, roaches 'n all, sure beats a hospital bed. But the hospital was where I stayed. An' stayed. All the leaves dropped. November blew in. I watched the 1980 Presidential Election on TV, shakin' my head the whole way. What's happened to the Democratic Party? They never woulda let that clown win in the old days. I, myself, sold my vote to my local ward boss for years. Sometimes, if they thought the election might be a little too close for comfort, they enlisted my assistance an' I'd go vote in several precincts in honor of devoted Chicago Democrats who couldn't make it to the polls in person on accounta bein' dead. I picked up a few extra bucks an' the Democratic Party beat the pants off those rich bastards like they're supposed to. That election made turnin' on the TV even more depressing, so I stopped watchin' it altogether an' took to starin' blank-like out the window. I figured they'd like that, the hospital people. It'd fit right in with their picture of old age. But my doctor got kinda worried by it. I guess he was afraid I was gonna kick, an' he'd lose credit for my miraculous recovery, so he bustled his fanny in an' told me I could go home at the end of the week. Happy? I wanna tell ya. I coulda kissed that little sonofabitch. Soon as I got settled back in my room at the Rienzi, cold weather or no cold weather, I was goin' straight to the Breslers on the corner of Clark 'n Diversey for an ice cream. Then I'd take my suits over to Arnold's tailoring shop to get another tuck took in 'em— I weigh less without my left lung. An' if I'm in real good workin' order, I'll walk over to the newsstand where everybody's sweetheart works, an' she'll tell me, "Whenever you get to feelin' down, look up."

MALE VOICE. Where do you live, Mr. Ponazecki?

MR. PONAZECKI *(to doctor)*. Huh? Whuzzat? *(To audience.)* I'm embarrassed. I wasn't payin' attention.

MALE VOICE. I-said...

MR. PONAZECKI *(to audience)*. He starts talkin' real loud, rollin' the words around on his tongue until they're good 'n wet.

MALE VOICE. I-said-Mis-ter-Po-na-zeck-i-Where-do-you-live?

MR. PONAZECKI *(to audience)*. I'm tempted to ask him to repeat that, but I don't want him to bust a blood vessel. *(To doctor.)* I live over to the Hotel Rienzi over on Diversey, right there where Clark 'n Broadway 'n Diversey all come together. You prob'ly drive by it sometimes. It's only a coupla blocks northa here. *(To audience.)* He's got this funny look on his face, like I'm talkin' to him in a foreign language or somethin'. An' he thinks I'm dim.

MALE VOICE. Mr. Ponazecki, hasn't anyone told you?

MR. PONAZECKI *(to audience)*. What? Told me what? *(To doctor.)* I guess not, Doc. What's to tell me?

MALE VOICE. It's gone.

MR. PONAZECKI *(to audience)*. He's lookin' real uncomfortable, almost sad. He's bleedin' for me.

MALE VOICE. Mr. Ponazecki, I hate to be the one to tell you this, but that old hotel and all the stores around it—the Walgreens, the currency exchange, that Chinese restaurant—they're all gone. They've been torn down. There's just a big hole there. A-big-hole-Mister-Ponazecki.

MR. PONAZECKI *(to audience)*. Didn't he think I heard him?

MALE VOICE. They're building a high-rise there, I think.

MR. PONAZECKI *(to audience)*. Suddenly I don't feel so energetic. Maybe one lung ain't enough after all. I'm an old man.

MALE VOICE. Yes, please do sit down, Mr. Ponazecki. Let me just ring for the nurse. We'll give you a little something to help you rest. This won't seem so horrible in the morning.

MR. PONAZECKI *(to audience)*. Who's he kiddin'?

MALE VOICE. I'm sure everyone who lives—lived—in that hotel has been placed in comparable surroundings.

MR. PONAZECKI *(to audience)*. Riverview Amusement Park. The streetcars. The Century. The Stockyards. Now they even got the Rienzi. Not even the poor ole Rienzi was safe. I guess somebody's always gotta get hurt by Progress. This time around it was my turn. Me 'n everybody who thought they could call the Rienzi home till they carried us outta there in a box. But Progress don't like to wait. The city wanted to spruce up that corner—gettin' ridda us was part of it, I bet, but they never say that. They said us old residents would get first crack at some cheap apartments they was settin' aside in the new high-rise goin' up where the Rienzi used to be—since we was "displaced"—but it'd be a while before they got it built. All I wanted was to move back to the old Rienzi—but I couldn't. The day I finally got bounced outta the hospital, I got placed in a transient hotel over by the Belmont L station. All hoursa the night I wake up from the trains. Kids throw bottles against the building an' carry on, usin' language my father woulda killed me if he ever even heard me thinkin' it.

MALE VOICE. Hey, fuckwad, I'm talkin' to you!

MR. PONAZECKI. The place hasn't been painted since the Korean War an' the roaches run faster'n the water. A coupla rooms upstairs rent by the hour. Don't get me wrong. I'm no prude. I'm all for free enterprise. But, Jesus, every night I lay there expectin' them bedsprings to come right through the ceiling 'n land on my head. I dunno. It's only about a mile, maybe less if you're a pigeon, to where the Rienzi used to be, but it's a whole other world. At least it is to me. Nobody knows me on Belmont. At the Shop 'n Save on Diversey all the checkers know me. I flirt with 'em. Tell 'em they're beautiful, especially if they're not. On Belmont everybody's Oriental or Arab or Mexican. They may be real nice people—if they're legal, they're prob'ly Democrats—but they're nobody I grew old with. There's a loud rock bar on Belmont by the L. Makes me afraid to be out too late. Hell, I'm scared when it's light. I'd get nervous over on Diversey, especially at night, but I was never afraid. Bein' afraid, knowin' you can't protect yourself, is hard to get used to for a guy who used to run a sandblaster. I thought maybe I could find some of my buddies from the Rienzi, so I called around, but they been scattered to the wind. Frank finally had to go live with his daughter in Des Plaines who can't stand the way he eats. Norman died of a stroke a coupla days before they were gonna make him move. Wilma finally had to break down 'n go in the nursing home after she swore she never would.

FEMALE VOICE. You'll never catch me goin' in no nursin' home. I'd take poison first.

MR. PONAZECKI. But she's got veins in her legs as thick as a rope. She couldn'ta lived anyplace but the Rienzi where she had friends to run her errands for her. A coupla the boys were placed in the same transient hotel way far west out by Six Corners. I'm glad for them they got placed together, but I'll never see 'em again. Everybody else, all my friends, scattered to the wind. Gone without a trace. Least no trace I could find. On a nice day—it's chilly, but I'm bundled—I decide to walk over to the Clark bus an' take it to Diversey. It's not far to Diversey, but I can't walk it. I wish I could. I hate the bus. It's so expensive anymore, even with my senior citizen discount, but what I really dread worst about it is gettin' on. I hafta grab holda the rail with both hands 'n hoist myself up a step at a time while everybody behind me waits. Same for gettin' off.

MALE VOICE. Jesus, I haven't got all day. Somebody give him a boost.

MR. PONAZECKI. I hafta take my time while everybody behind me taps their feet 'n sighs real loud. But I'm lonely. I wanna see the hole. I get off at Clark 'n Diversey, an' I stop in at that coffee shop next to the Parkway movie theater, the Super Bowl Grill, to sit 'n catch my breath, but nothin' looks good to me, so I leave without spendin' a cent. Walkin' slow, I cross the street to take a look. There's fenced boardwalk all the way around, an' a coupla men are leanin' there watchin' a bulldozer splash through a big dirty poola water down in this gigantic hole where I used to live. They tell me I shoulda been there to see the buildings pulled down.

MALE VOICE. The wrecking crew'd stop for the night, sometimes right in the middla wreckin' a room, an' there'd be this lonely-lookin' sink hangin' there, three stories up with no room around it, just air. Looked pretty funny, somebody's sink just hangin' there. You shoulda seen it.

MR. PONAZECKI *(to MALE VOICE)*. I'm glad I didn't. *(To audience.)* One of 'em circles the side of his head with his finger like I'm blind an' can't see he thinks I'm crazy. Wait a few years, buddy. Your turn's comin'. I try to walk away with my dignity, but I catch my foot 'n fall. This friendly fem guy helps me up. The neighborhood's full of 'em anymore, but I don't mind 'em. I guess the city don't either. I'm the one they moved to Belmont, not him.

MALE VOICE. Are you okay, mister?

MR. PONAZECKI. I tell him I am, but I'm not. My knees buckle again an' when I wake up, I'm back in the hospital. An' I'm glad.

END

THE MEMORY CLUB OF AMERICA
by
Nicole J. Burton

CHARACTERS

MARCUS CEDARBLADE: Mid-40s, university museum director, pushy, and hopelessly forgetful. Remembers whole new things, makes up historical facts. President of the club.

DENA DOBSON: Early 50s, a professor of mathematics. Much loved by students. Forgets to give tests and pick up assignments, but never forgets a football game. Secretary of the club.

JOHNNY 'BUG' JOHNSON: About 50 and loaded with energy, a real club man. Sanitary supervisor with the Baton Rouge Department of Public Works. Good on details; forgets the big event. Got his nickname after an unfortunate locker-room incident in high school. It stuck. Member of the club.

Note: Multi-ethnic casting preferred.

PLACE: A large meeting room in the local public library.

TIME: The present.

THE MEMORY CLUB OF AMERICA

SETTING: *In the library, books on the shelves and portraits of Huey Long, General G.T. Beauregard, and former President George Bush on the walls. [When Black actors are cast, upon entering, one of them flips the Beauregard portrait over to reveal a portrait of Martin Luther King.]*

AT RISE: *MARCUS CEDARBLADE, DENA DOBSON and JOHNNY 'BUG' JOHNSON enter and prepare to sit down around a table. BUG sets up the portable lectern and the club banner that is emblazoned with "The Memory Club of America" and the MCA motto: "We Live In the Present."*

MARCUS *(standing and rapping the gavel on the lectern).* I'd like to call this meeting to order. Welcome to the monthly meeting of the Memory Club of America, Baton Rouge chapter. The first item on the agenda is old business. Would you please read the minutes from the last meeting, Lena?

DENA. Dena. I thought we were going to skip the minutes. I have to leave early for a faculty meeting.

MARCUS. Just read the minutes.

DENA *(standing).* The last meeting was held on August 10th. It was a hot night and the air-conditioning was broken so we met at Ed's Seafood, that's at the corner of Beauregard and LaSalle...

MARCUS. We know where Ed's is—we were there.

DENA. Ralph gave a report on the MCA abridged books project, which is helping high school students develop a love of literature. He read us the *Moby Dick* abridgment, and I would like to quote it in full because I think this is the wave of the future in our hectic society...

MARCUS. Get on with the minutes.

DENA. Whatever I take down is the minutes, and stop interrupting me or I'll file a complaint with the national office!

MARCUS. And what will you say? My brother-in-law got on my tail for being a long-winded, self-absorbed...

DENA. For breaking one of the traditions of our organization, namely, no interrupting. "Interrupting others is a symptom of our disease. We try always to encourage a fellowship of listening in all our activities." Tradition 7. As I was saying, *Moby Dick*: *(She reads.)* "Moby Dick was a great white whale that Captain Ahab tried to kill. He did not succeed, and eventually, he died. In the process, he learned that the struggle for life..." *(She makes one of her signature extemporaneous digressions.)* ...is equal to or greater than the sum of the three angles of an isosceles triangle, and furthermore, according to Plato, the Shadow World is merely a reflection of the actual world beyond. Thank you. *(She sits down.)*

MARCUS *(wearily)*. Finish the minutes.

BUG. You were getting ready to talk about the elections today. The absentee ballots. *(He waves a bundle of ballots at her, encouragingly.)*

DENA *(stands)*. Oh, yes. The amended bylaws permit voting by mail, and members were instructed to send their ballots to Bug Johnson if they were not planning to vote in person. You have the absentee ballots?

BUG. Right here.

DENA. Thank you. The candidates for office of the Baton Rouge chapter of the Memory Club of America are— President: Marcus Cedarblade, current President; and Dena Dobson, current Secretary/Treasurer. Vice-President for Education: Louis Mirabeau and Neville Barbary. Neville is the former treasurer but had to quit when his wife left him. It was a terrible shame and a scandal, because she left him for the soccer coach of the Catholic Junior League over at Ponchatoula. How they came to meet...

BUG. Dena. You're digressing again. Pick up at the secretary/treasurer.

MARCUS. And read from your notes.

DENA. Secretary/Treasurer: Bug Johnson, unopposed. Now I shall hand out the ballots. *(She does.)* Do either of you need me to repeat the list of candidates?

BUG. No, ma'am. I wrote them down right here. *(They work on their ballots.)*

DENA. When you have completed your ballots, pass them to Bug. *(They do.)* And while Bug is counting, I'll turn the meeting over to you, Mr. President.

MARCUS. Thank you. We have one item of new business. How's the draft of our manual coming, Bart?

DENA. Bug's counting. What else do you have?

MARCUS. That's it.

DENA. What about this month's pnumatic device?

MARCUS. Mne-mon-ic.

DENA. Mnemonic, demonic, I can never remember them.

MARCUS. This month's mnemonic device helps us prepare for the fall time change: Spring Forward, Fall Back. In the spring, we move the clocks forward...

DENA. I know that, but what makes it pnumatic?

MARCUS. 'Cause it helps us remember which way to turn the clocks.

BUG. I got 'em.

DENA. Are you sure you counted right?

BUG. It's only eight ballots.

MARCUS. Are you ready to announce the results?

BUG. Yes, sir. The results of the 1990 general election of the Baton Rouge chapter of the Memory Club...are you taking this down?

DENA. I've got it. The Baton Rouge chapter of the...

BUG. You weren't writing it down. Written reminders are the keystone of our recovery. "If it's not written, it's rotten." All right. The election results are...for Secretary/Treasurer, Bug Johnson. *(Grins and waits.)* Aren't you going to give me a round of applause?

MARCUS. Read the results.

BUG *(sulking)*. We used to give all the winners their own round of applause.

DENA *(clapping)*. Congratulations, Bug!

BUG. Thank you. I'm very honored. And for the position of Vice-President of Education it's a tie between Louis and Neville. We'll have to hold a run-off election, won't we, Mr. President?

MARCUS. Yes. Keep reading.

BUG. And for the position of President of the Baton Rouge chapter... *(MARCUS and DENA sit forward in their chairs.)* ...of the Memory Club of America, it gives me great pleasure to announce that we have a definite winner...

MARCUS. Who is it?!

BUG. And the winner is...Dena Dobson. First female chapter president in the history of MCA! *(Clapping.)* Congratulations, Dena! *(DENA is radiant; MARCUS is stormy.)*

MARCUS. I demand a recount!

BUG. I already counted them twice. This is your pile, this is Dena's, and one's a write-in.

MARCUS. A what?

BUG. A write-in vote.

MARCUS. Who did they write in?

BUG. Wayne Newton. Pretty clear whose vote that is.

MARCUS. Damn Gretchen! What an imbecile. Before I go I want to say...take this down, Madam Secretary/Treasurer. I want these words written 'cause they're going to come back to haunt us. I think electing a woman as president of a chapter of the Memory Club of America is a perverse mistake.

DENA. Wait a minute!

MARCUS. I'll tell you why. A woman cannot possibly represent the truly recollection deficient in modern society. How many notable women have there been who have suffered from this affliction? *(Pause.)* No Einsteins, no Edisons, not even a Samuel Goldwyn. Oh,

The Memory Club of America

women suffer age-related memory loss the same as men, but they've got less to forget in the first place! How hard is it to buy groceries, put on makeup, or teach a bunch of second graders? No, it's men who suffer from this disease, not only because it's us who lose our minds so tragically and in such great numbers, but because we make the great contributions to mankind, and our loss is a blow against the entire race. For a woman to represent what is in essence a man's disease is, well, it's like electing a woman to be president of Impotents Anonymous. I move we change the bylaws to prohibit women from holding the office of president. *(He sits down.)*

DENA *(stands)*. Fellow members. I am honored to be elected the first female chapter president in the history of our organization. *(She reads.)* "Recollection deficiency is the fastest-growing disease in this country, afflicting hundreds of thousands of otherwise lucid, active people of all ages. The Memory Club of America does not discriminate on the basis of race, religion, or psychological profile, bylaws, part 2." *(To MARCUS.)* You should be ashamed of yourself. There are plenty of reasons why having a woman president may even improve the club. First, we women understand this disease because we have to live with so many of you who suffer from it. Second, there have been plenty of recollection-deficient women throughout history. What about Catherine the Great? Nancy Reagan? Little Bo Peep? And who has not known that abyss into which we all sink, sooner or later, saying, "I know that name, I know that face, who the hell is it?" But when Ptolemy cried out, "Is there no easier way to learn?" Euclid replied, "There is no royal road to geometry." With the help of the Memory Club of America, we learn to do our best with what we have, to be free to live our lives in the present, and to be joyful whether our family and friends remember to show up or not. So I say to you in the spirit of harmony, brother Bug and Marcus, live in the present. Follow your bliss. And thank you for your support. *(She sits down. BUG claps.)*

MARCUS. Is there any more new business?

DENA. Yes. I want to remind everyone to "Spring back and Fall forward."

MARCUS. That's "Spring forward and Fall back."

DENA. I know, *(Broad gestures.)* "Spring forward and Fall down." *(Grabbing BUG and MARCUS by the hand.)* Isn't it wonderful how we're getting so much better?

MARCUS *(gavel)*. This meeting is adjourned.

END

A MAN AND HIS PLANT
by
D.M. Bocaz-Larson

CHARACTERS

HOOPER: An elderly man who is poor, but happy, in his small apartment that is decorated with one very special plant.

MRS. CREB: A snoopy old woman who lives in the building with Hooper. She is cranky and very critical with a permanently sour look. She neither understands nor approves of Hooper's way of life.

MRS. ARNOLD: A new addition to the building who unfortunately gets mixed up with Mrs. Creb. Mrs. Arnold is a kind woman who is tolerant of Hooper's eccentric nature, but also tolerant of the nature of every other person around her.

MAIL PERSON: The new mail carrier for the building whom Hooper invites to tea.

BEN ARNOLD JR.: Mrs. Arnold's son who takes an avid interest in Hooper's plant.

Note: All characters, including Hooper, can be played by either men or women.

PLACE: An apartment building for the elderly.

TIME: The present.

A MAN AND HIS PLANT

SCENE ONE

SETTING: *Lights come up on a simply decorated apartment for the elderly. The room consists of a living room (sofa, table, and chair) which doubles as a bedroom, and a kitchenette, UL. The bathroom is through a door, L. The door to the outside hallway is UR. There is also a coat rack, DR. And proudly displayed DL, is an ugly potted weed that sits upon a pedestal.*

AT RISE: *The UR door opens and HOOPER enters happily with a grocery bag. He leaves his door open so people feel welcome.*

HOOPER. Ah, what a beautiful day. Not a drop of rain hit this old grey head. *(He crosses to kitchenette with bag where he sets it down. He speaks to someone apparently offstage.)* I think I remembered everything you asked for, plus a few extras that were on sale. *(Takes coat to coat rack.)* I know, I know. No extras. We can't afford it, but I figured they were deals a human couldn't pass by. *(Crosses slowly back to kitchenette.)* It truly was a fine day. I know I always say that, but it truly was today. The park was at its best. *(Dreamily.)* It sorta...I don't know...sparkled today. Frank even gave me a free hot dog for lunch. "Just because it's a good day," he said. I know. It *must* be a pretty good day when Frank gives out free hot dogs. Oh, and the best thing happened since I've been volunteering to clean up the park. *(Proudly.)* The mayor personally came to thank me for keeping the park clean. *(Pause.)* Well, the mayor was there for a press thingamajig, but he did thank me. *(Thoughtfully.)* He even had pictures taken of us shakin' hands. Then, he mumbled about remembering to do something on such-and-such a day, and went on. *(Unloads groceries.)* I got some cherry soda water for me. I always need something a little special. And for you. I got some super enriched fertilizer! *(Takes out fertilizer and crosses to plant.)* I know you told me not to get it, but I also know you really wanted it. You think you can fool me, but I can read between the lines. Body language is my specialty. *(Sets fertilizer down and continues to unpack bag.)* After work, I stayed awhile to feed plants, as usual, and lo and behold those darn city workers pulled up all the weeds in the flower bed again. Don't they know those weeds are important? The park's becoming less and less natural every day. But don't worry. I buried the weeds in the flower beds again. They'll sprout up in no time. *(At bottom of bag.)* The final specialty of the day was something I couldn't pass up. It's a new white pot for my best pal. *(Takes the pot to his weed.)* Between the pot and super fertilizer, you'll feel like a young sprout again. *(Goes to coat.)* Oh, yes. I remembered a paper, too. *(Takes it from his coat pocket and unrolls it.)* It's yesterday's paper, but it didn't cost anything. Joe always leaves the leftovers out for whoever wants 'em the next day. *(Takes a chair and sits next to plant. Flips through paper.)* I'll skip all the boring stuff...oh, heh. Here's something. *(Reads squinty-eyed and with some difficulty. He never was really taught to read.)* "R-ain F-orests of...South A-merica...are being...cut down." Uh... *(Struggling with words.)* "Cure for a...di-sease may be..." *(He shows paper to plant.)* What's this word... *(Listens to plant. Tries to sound out word.)* Dis...disappearing. *(Nods.)* Thanks. "...disappearing...each day." Wow. That's rough. Isn't it horrible to hear about all those plants being killed? It's even more upsetting if they might do people some good, like cure a sickness... *(Thinking of an example.)* ...or a disease like skin cancer. But, with all those plants and trees disappearing, I guess we'll never know. *(Looks at plant.)* I don't know what I'd do if I didn't have you anymore. You've been so good to me. *(Touches his cheek, distant.)* You've stuck with me through everything...I really don't know how I could have got along without you.

(MRS. CREB has been spying at the door with MRS. ARNOLD, who reluctantly does so.)

HOOPER. Well, that's enough news for now. Let's skip to the comics. We can read the rest later. *(Looks for comics.)*
MRS. CREB *(pointing. Loud whisper)*. That's Hooper.
MRS. ARNOLD. He doesn't look too strange.
MRS. CREB. He talks to a weed! And a very ugly one at that. I can't even see why he has the thing, let alone talks to it.

A Man and His Plant 57

MRS. ARNOLD. People talk to plants all the time.

MRS. CREB. But I'm sure they don't hold whole conversations with them.

MRS. ARNOLD. So what if they don't. That doesn't mean Mr. Hooper can't.

MRS. CREB. I don't know. It's weird. That's all.

HOOPER *(notices them)*. Mrs. Crab! *(Gets up. Welcoming her.)* How nice of you to come by!

MRS. CREB. I was just showing Mrs. Arnold the building. We merely paused a moment at your door. We must be going...

HOOPER *(goes to them. Brings MRS. ARNOLD in)*. Nice to meet you, Mrs. Arnold. New to the building?

MRS. CREB. Of course she's new. You would have seen her before if she weren't.

HOOPER. Care for some tea, Mrs. Arnold?

MRS. CREB. No, we must be going.

HOOPER *(pleasantly)*. I didn't ask you, did I, Mrs. Crab?

MRS. CREB. It's Mrs. Creb.

HOOPER. Well, I'm asking you to tea, also. Please. Come sit down. *(Escorts MRS. ARNOLD to sofa.)*

MRS. ARNOLD. Thank you, Mr. Hooper. *(MRS. CREB sits on sofa with her while HOOPER gets tea. Whispers to MRS. CREB.)* He's not so strange.

HOOPER. Do you like your tea in fat or skinny cups?

MRS. CREB *(to MRS. ARNOLD)*. Just wait. You'll see.

HOOPER. Skinny it is. *(He pours two cups for tea.)* You're going to love this tea. It's good stuff. *(Gives them each a cup.)*

MRS. ARNOLD. Thank you. *(They drink and then look oddly at their cups.)*

MRS. CREB. This is iced tea!

HOOPER *(concerned)*. Isn't that what everyone drinks in the summertime?

MRS. CREB. Yes, but it's not summer anymore. It's fall.

HOOPER. Well, I've had the tea since summer. *(MRS. ARNOLD smiles and drinks her tea.)* Would you like to meet my friend, Mrs. Arnold?

MRS. CREB *(smiles evilly)*. Of course she would, Hooper.

HOOPER *(takes MRS. ARNOLD happily over to plant)*. Mrs. Arnold, this is my friend, 32nd Street.

MRS. ARNOLD. 32nd Street?

HOOPER. I found her in an empty lot there. I couldn't think of anything better.

MRS. ARNOLD. Hello, 32nd Street.

HOOPER. You really don't have to say her name. She always seems to know when you're speaking to her. *(He studies a mark on MRS. ARNOLD's face. He whispers something to 32nd Street about the mark and looks as if he's trying to figure something out about it.)*

MRS. CREB. Sorry to rush off, Hooper. But, we must be going.

HOOPER *(remembers now)*. That's it! That's what that is. I knew I'd seen it before. *(Stops them.)* Mrs. Arnold?

MRS. ARNOLD. Yes?

HOOPER. You have skin cancer, don't you?

MRS. ARNOLD *(self-consciously touches her face)*. Yes.

HOOPER. I had it, too. But, it's all gone, now.

MRS. CREB. All gone? How?

HOOPER *(goes to plant)*. She helped me.

MRS. CREB. Come on, Hooper. This is going too far.

MRS. ARNOLD *(interested, goes to him)*. How did she help? *(HOOPER takes a fallen leaf from the plant's pot and gives it to her. She holds it before her.)*

HOOPER. Take it and rub it on the spots of skin cancer. *(She reluctantly does so. They pause a moment.)*

MRS. CREB. This is nonsense. Come along, Mrs. Arnold.

MRS. ARNOLD *(touches spot)*. It feels kind of funny.

MRS. CREB. The weed has probably made it worse. *(Takes MRS. ARNOLD to door.)* Let's go. *(They exit.)*

HOOPER *(to plant)*. Thank you for the leaf. That should make Mrs. Arnold happy. *(Pause. Sits next to plant.)* Frank gave me a bad time about my volunteer work at the park. He says a person works to get money. What I do doesn't make any sense to him. I told him I worked my whole life just as hard, if not harder, than any other guy without an education. I'd get my pay, and before I knew it, it would be gone. I could never even dream of having a family because of how much everything cost. I didn't even like my job. All day long, I was an ever-moving part of that big machine. Lift the metal, push it through. Lift the metal, push it through. It got really boring. But I had to keep a roof over my head, and food in my fridge. *(Pause.)* Thank goodness I didn't have a family. *(Pause. [Note: optional dialog may be used for a female character. For example: Pick out the bad peaches, let the good ones go by, etc.].)* Well, I told Frank that I'm happy cleaning the park and my life is good. No more machine. Only happiness. He said he couldn't see how I could be happy having so little. But I didn't quite understand, because I have so much. *(Returns to paper.)* Now for the comics. *(Lights fade to black.)*

SCENE TWO

(A MAIL PERSON appears at the door, looking for a mail slot. HOOPER goes to him, welcoming.)

HOOPER. Hello, friend. Can I help you with something?
MAIL PERSON. Well, uh...
HOOPER. Don't stand out in the hall. Come in and relax. I'll get you some tea. *(Goes to get some.)*
MAIL PERSON *(still at door)*. I still have a lot of mail to deliver. I just couldn't find where to put your mail.
HOOPER. Fat or skinny cup?
MAIL PERSON *(gives in)*. Skinny.
HOOPER *(takes cup to him)*. I don't have a mail thing anymore. *(Takes him to sofa.)* Please, come sit down.
MAIL PERSON *(goes to sofa and sits)*. What happened to your mailbox?
HOOPER. I took it down.
MAIL PERSON. Why?
HOOPER. I want to get to know people. The world isn't as kind as it used to be. People figure ways to make things go faster. They work out the best way to save time. No one talks anymore. No one listens. They just rush on, and on, and on...

MAIL PERSON *(sets down tea)*. Thank you for the tea. I must be going.

HOOPER. Already?

MAIL PERSON. Here's your mail. *(Hands it to him. HOOPER searches through it for something, but doesn't find it.)*

HOOPER. Darn it. It hasn't come yet. Darn, darn, darn.

MAIL PERSON. What are you looking for?

HOOPER. I entered a mail-in plant contest. You just send in a picture of your plant and the best lookin' one wins a year's supply of Johnson's fertilizer. The suspense is killing me. Oh, how rude of me. Would you like to meet my plant?

MAIL PERSON *(anxious to leave)*. I really have to go. *(HOOPER takes him to plant.)*

HOOPER This is my friend, 32nd Street. *(Aside.)* That's where I found her. *(To plant.)* And this is our new mail person ... uh ... did you say your name?

MAIL PERSON. Tony. *(Looks oddly at plant.)*

HOOPER *(to plant)*. This is Tony.

MAIL PERSON *(reluctantly)*. Uh, hi.

HOOPER. Isn't she a beauty?

MAIL PERSON *(thinks HOOPER is very strange)*. Breathtaking.

HOOPER. Did you hear that? He said "breathtaking"!

MAIL PERSON. I've got to go. Thank you for the tea. *(He exits quickly.)*

HOOPER Bye. Thank you for dropping by. *(To plant.)* Nice kid, that mail person. I hope the contest results come back soon. *(Clears cups from table.)* So many guests lately. We're a popular couple of life forms.

(MRS. ARNOLD and MRS. CREB rush in. MRS. ARNOLD is ecstatic.)

MRS. ARNOLD. Mr. Hooper! You've performed a miracle!
HOOPER *(calmly)*. Hello, Mrs. Arnold. Mrs. Crab.
MRS. CREB. Creb.
MRS. ARNOLD *(goes to him)*. Look at where you had me rub that leaf. *(He does and smiles.)* The spot's are almost gone.
HOOPER. Yep. Clears right up with a little dab. The doctor told me that I didn't have long to live after I got those cancer spots. He called it... *(Struggling with word.)* Malig... Maligna...
MRS. ARNOLD *(knowing the word too well)*. Malignant melanoma.
HOOPER. Yeah. It's supposed to spread through your innards like crazy. But my plant stood by me the whole time until the stuff was gone. *(Pause. Thinks.)* Ya know. I haven't heard from that doctor for a long time. *(Goes to plant, speaks to it.)* I guess he figures I must be dead. We sure put one over on him.
MRS. ARNOLD. This is incredible. The doctors told me it was probably too late, but now...
MRS. CREB. How come you've never told anyone about this?
HOOPER. I don't know. No one has ever asked.
MRS. CREB *(angrily)*. People can die from what you two had! Don't you want people to live?!
HOOPER. Mrs. Crab. My friend does what she pleases. It's not up to me to decide who she helps or doesn't help.

MRS. CREB. You're insane. It's just a weed. It has no feelings!

HOOPER *(hurt)*. That's not a nice thing to say about someone's best friend. Especially when she's in the same room.

MRS. CREB. You're hopeless, Hooper.

MRS. ARNOLD. My son was helping me move in today. He works for one of the big medical labs. I asked him to come down and look at your plant. *(To MRS. CREB.)* Plants are his specialty.

HOOPER *(puzzled)*. Why? Does he have skin cancer, too?

MRS. CREB. Your weed cures skin cancer, you idiot!

HOOPER. So?

MRS. CREB. He'll probably want to see what kind of plant it is so they can get more.

HOOPER. Oh. Well, I showed it to the man at the plant store and he said it's been wiped out just about everywhere. Nobody liked them very much. *(Speaks gently to plant.)* It's kind of sad to be one of the last of your kind.

(Enter BEN ARNOLD.)

BEN. Is this the place?

MRS. ARNOLD. Yes. Come in. Hooper, this is my son Ben Jr. *(They shake hands.)*

HOOPER. Hi, would you like some tea?

BEN. No, thanks.

MRS. CREB. The weed is over there. *(BEN goes to plant. HOOPER follows closely.)*

BEN *(examines it)*. I'm not sure I recognize what it is... *(Looks closely at a leaf and plucks it off.)*

HOOPER *(jumps between BEN and plant)*. Hey, watch it! *(Whispers gently to plant.)*

BEN *(ignoring him)*. Oh, my word. It can't be.

MRS. CREB. What? What's wrong?

BEN. This is bad.

MRS. CREB. What?!

BEN. It's Tauschia tenuissima. Farmers called it a pest. It was one of the first pests that they used weed killers to destroy. There are hardly any of these left, if any at all. And if it is actually a cure... we can't risk losing it. *(Goes to HOOPER and takes out checkbook.)* How much for your plant?

HOOPER *(shocked)*. What?

BEN. Ten. Twenty dollars?

HOOPER *(shields plant)*. You're asking me to sell her?

MRS. CREB. Yes, Hooper. I would do it if I were you.

BEN. Forty dollars?

HOOPER. No!

MRS. CREB. You need the money, Hooper. Take it.

BEN. Fifty dollars?

HOOPER. You're asking me to sell my best friend? That's sick!

BEN. Seventy-five dollars?

MRS. ARNOLD. This is important, Mr. Hooper. It's for the greater good.

BEN. Eighty dollars?

HOOPER. Greater good?! Humans have killed enough plants already! Why should I let them kill them all?!

A Man and His Plant

MRS. CREB. Sell the plant, Hooper!

BEN. One hundred dollars?

MRS. ARNOLD. Please, Mr. Hooper.

HOOPER *(picks up plant and holds her).* You can't have her! She's not for sale!

BEN *(frustrated).* Two hundred dollars?

MRS. CREB. You hear that, Hooper? That's a whole lot of money.

HOOPER *(really upset).* No, I won't do it! I won't sell her!

BEN. Three hundred?

HOOPER. No!

MRS. CREB. Come out of happy land, Hooper! You need the money! It's only a stupid weed, for heaven's sake!

HOOPER *(angry. Sets down plant).* Only a stupid weed? She means more to me than anything else in this world! She'll never leave me. She'll never call me a bum. She loves me for what I am and asks for nothing more than love in return. Now, you want to kill her! Cut her up! Pluck off her leaves! *(Takes leaf from BEN.)* Get out, you fiends! *(Shoos them away.)* Let us live in peace! *(They exit. Goes to plant.)* I would never let them take you from me. *(Pets her.)* Never. *(Lights fade to black.)*

SCENE THREE

(Lights come up on the same scene except for the plant which is gone. HOOPER enters happily. [Note: The scene change needs to be quick so the flow of the play isn't interrupted. This can be done by having a place to hide the plant onstage and positioning HOOPER in the room as the scene begins.].)

HOOPER. Ah, what a beautiful day. Better than yesterday, by far. *(Goes to hang up coat.)* You should have seen it. The birds were singing, the sun shone brightly in the sky, and there was a pleasant little breeze that... *(Sees plant is missing. He goes white, drops coat, and runs to empty pedestal.)* What...what... *(Breathes heavily.)* Where are you? *(Pause. Frantically moves around.)* What's going on? *(Stops.)* Did I move you? *(Tries to smile.)* Are you hiding from me? *(Pause. Scared.)* Where are you? *(Yells.)* What's going on?!

(MRS. CREB appears at the door.)

MRS. CREB. I helped them take it, Hooper. They need that plant more than you do.
HOOPER *(softly)*. What?
MRS. CREB. I called Ben while you were gone, and some people from his lab came and got it.
HOOPER. What...

MRS. CREB. I did it for your own good. You have almost no money to your name. You need the money Ben offered you.

HOOPER *(lost)*. But...she was my friend.

MRS. CREB. They left a check for you. That should keep you company for a while.

HOOPER. I don't want a check! I want her!

MRS. CREB. Take part of the money and buy some more.

HOOPER. There aren't any more. Humans destroyed them all.

MRS. CREB. Quit feeling sorry for yourself and take the money. *(Hands him check. He won't take it. She stuffs it in his pocket. He takes it out and rips it up.)* What are you doing? That was for five hundred dollars! *(Picks up pieces where he threw them on the floor. Pause.)* You really are crazy, aren't you? *(Stands up. Angrily.)* That plant can save people's lives and you wanted to keep it all for yourself. I couldn't stand by and watch you keep people from getting a cure for a fatal disease. Besides, you know you can use the money.

HOOPER. I don't want their dirty money!

MRS. CREB. Fine! Starve to death for all I care! *(Holds up pieces of check.)* Now, you have nothing. No plant, no money. Nothing.

(She starts to exit. MRS. ARNOLD enters.)

MRS. ARNOLD *(sadly)*. Hooper? *(MRS. CREB stops to listen. HOOPER sits at empty pedestal and says nothing. MRS. ARNOLD crosses to him.)* Hooper. I have some bad news. *(He is silent.)* Your plant, 32nd Street, is dead. *(He bows his head. Shattered by this final blow.)*

MRS. CREB. Dead?

MRS. ARNOLD. They got it to the lab and it just wilted and died. They can't figure out why.

HOOPER. They're all gone, now. No plant, no cure. Nothing.

MRS. ARNOLD. Hooper... I... thought it was the right thing to do. I'm sorry.

HOOPER *(looks up sadly)*. I'm sorry, too, Mrs. Arnold. Good-bye.

MRS. ARNOLD. Let's leave him alone.

MRS. CREB. Gladly. *(CREB exits. MRS. ARNOLD stays a moment.)*

MRS. ARNOLD. Hooper... is there anything I can do?

HOOPER. No, Mrs. Arnold. Enough has been done already.

MRS. ARNOLD. I feel so bad about what's happened... I wish I could... *(So upset she becomes silent.)*

HOOPER. Could I be alone for a while, Mrs. Arnold?

MRS. ARNOLD. Sure, Mr. Hooper. I'm sorry. *(Starts to leave.)*

HOOPER. Mrs. Arnold?

MRS. ARNOLD. Yes?

HOOPER. My door is always open.

MRS. ARNOLD *(smiles)*. Thank you. *(Exits.)*

HOOPER *(pause. Looks at table)*. I'm sorry I couldn't stop them. I did almost everything I could. I hated to lock the door. It would have been so unfriendly of me, but still, maybe I should have. *(HOOPER rubs his hand along the top of the pedestal where the plant was.)* I'm so very sorry. *(His hand stops. He feels something odd on top of the pedestal. Curiously he picks something very small up with his fingers. It's a tiny seed. Pause.)* Seeds! She had babies! *(Excitedly he fills the new white pot with spare soil at hand and goes back to pedestal. Arranges seeds.)* One, two, three. Wow. Three babies. *(To seeds.)* I'll just have to plant you all, right away, won't I? *(Plants them.)* Here we go. One, two, three. *(Smiles.)* Oh, your mother will be so proud. Pretty soon, with a little care, you'll sprout right up. A little water. A little sun. And everything will be perfect. You'll like it here. Your mother always did. We had some good times. *(Pause.)* I'll never forget her. *(Pause.)* Now, you three behave and eat right. And if you all take care of yourselves, you'll grow up to be big, beautiful, and strong, just like your mother. *(Smiles happily as lights fade to black.)*

END

HORSESHOE BEND
by
Mark Plaiss

CHARACTERS

BILL
TOM
DAVE

PLACE: Tom's backyard, small town on Ohio River.

TIME: A July afternoon, the present.

HORSESHOE BEND

AT RISE: *BILL, TOM and DAVE sitting in backyard drinking beer.*

BILL. It's hot.
TOM. Damn hot.
DAVE. It's *July*.
BILL. How hot is it?
TOM. Hell hot.
DAVE. Ninety-four? Ninety-five?
TOM. Ninety-eight.
DAVE. Whatever.
BILL. After ninety-five, what's the difference?
DAVE. Don't know. Hundred's pretty hot.
TOM. Damn hot.
BILL. What'd we do before air-conditioning?
TOM. What'd we do?
BILL. Yeah.
TOM. I tell you what we did.
DAVE. What's that, Tom?
TOM. Suffered.
DAVE. You got that right.
TOM. Lying in bed at night, the window open...
BILL. ...no breeze...
TOM. ...no nothing, 'cept sweat pouring down your...
DAVE. ...crack!
BILL. Ohhhhh!

TOM. Praying, just praying...
BILL. ...for sleep.
DAVE. But will it come?
TOM, BILL, DAVE *(together)*. Nooooooo!
BILL. I hate summer.
TOM. Can you imagine what it must be like in Mississippi?
DAVE. Right now?
TOM. This very moment.
BILL. We don't have to live like this, you know.
DAVE. Like what?
BILL. Like *this*.
TOM. Could be worse.
BILL. *How?*
TOM. Could be in Mississippi.
BILL. Bet it's hot *there*.
TOM. Damn hot.
DAVE. Why do people live there?
BILL. Where they were born.
DAVE. But it's so hot.
BILL. Ever been there?
DAVE. No.
BILL. Think it's hotter there than here?
TOM. Well, get this.
BILL. What?
TOM. Knew a guy from Mississippi.
BILL. OK.
TOM. Fremil. Frank Fremil.
DAVE. Get out.
TOM. What?

DAVE. His name was *Frank Fremil?*
TOM. Yeah.
DAVE. So what did this Fremil guy do?
TOM. Sweated. A lot.
BILL. What was his *job*.
TOM. Sold cars.
DAVE. In the Magnolia state.
TOM. New Albany.
BILL. Mississippi?
TOM. That's the Magnolia state, Bill.
DAVE. So?
TOM. So he just up and moved.
BILL. From Mississippi.
TOM. Yeah.
DAVE. Why?
TOM. Guess.
BILL. Too hot?
TOM. Too *damn* hot.
BILL. Chew on this.
DAVE. What?
BILL. Mississippi. Mid-July. 1800s.
TOM. Talk about heat.
DAVE. No AC...
BILL. ...no fans...
TOM. ...no nothing, just...
BILL. ...agony...
DAVE. ...and B.O.
BILL. Don't even want to think about it.
TOM. Then think Minnesota.
BILL. There you go.

DAVE. Don't know.
BILL. What?
DAVE. Think Minnesota in *January*.
BILL. Let me ask you something.
DAVE. OK.
BILL. Think the coldest you've ever been.
DAVE. Soldier Field, Chicago. Bears and Packers.
TOM. December?
DAVE. January. Top row.
BILL. Could you have gotten warmer by putting on more clothes?
DAVE. I suppose.
BILL. Now. Think the hottest you ever been.
DAVE. Foley dormitory, IU. August. Room directly over boiler.
BILL. OK. If you'd stripped down—
DAVE. Naked?
BILL. Buck naked. Could you've gotten any cooler?
DAVE. I did, and I couldn't.
BILL. I rest my case.
DAVE. Even tried soaking towels in cold water then laying them over me...
BILL. Over you?
DAVE. ...yeah, while I tried to sleep.
BILL. No go?
DAVE. Utter failure.
BILL. That's some kinda hot.
TOM. But it's just not the heat, it's...
BILL. ...the humidity.
DAVE. Hate it.

BILL. Who *likes* it?
TOM. Know those people who are always talking about *dry* heat?
BILL. You mean like Arizona or something?
TOM. Yeah. Know what I tell 'em?
DAVE. What?
TOM. I tell 'em to go in the kitchen, crank the oven up to a hundred, and climb in.
DAVE. The *oven?*
TOM. No humidity.
BILL. Bingo.
DAVE. So you're telling me you'd rather die from cold than heat?
TOM. I didn't say that, but I would say that. Yeah.
DAVE. You would.
TOM. Where's the choice?
DAVE. Well—
TOM. What's the coldest cold?
BILL. Ice.
TOM. And the hottest hot?
BILL. Fire.
TOM. So, you just kinda drift off to sleep when you freeze.
DAVE. Kinda miserable beforehand, though.
TOM. Beats roasting before you burn.
BILL. Touché.
TOM. Face it, gentlemen, summertime in the Ohio River Valley equals...
BILL. ...Hazy...
DAVE. ...Hot...

TOM. ...and humid.
BILL. Three big Hs.
TOM. Minnesota equals cold in winter. Mississippi equals hot in summer.
BILL. Just depends on where you live.
DAVE. Everything's relative.
TOM. $E = MC^2$.
BILL. Know what sounds good?
DAVE. Sinatra singing "In the Way"?
TOM. "*All* the Way."
BILL. Another beer.
TOM. Think I'll go in and get one.
DAVE. I'm through.
BILL. Make it two.
TOM. *Ninety*-two. Oertles '92. Remember that?
DAVE. My grandfather's favorite beer.
BILL. Whatever happened to it?
DAVE. Beer that made Milwaukee famous.
BILL. That was Blatz.
TOM. Yes sir. Beer sure would hit the spot just about now.
BILL. Long as it's cold.
DAVE. Well, yeah.
TOM. Goes without saying.
DAVE. Who drinks warm beer?
TOM. Think I'll go get a cold one now.
DAVE. Blatz?
TOM. *Bud*.
BILL. Red White & Blue.
TOM. 'scuse me?

BILL. My uncle's favorite beer.
TOM. Red White & Blue.
DAVE. Good beer.
TOM. Yeah?
BILL. 'specially on the Fourth of July.
TOM. Yeah, think I'll go right in there—
BILL *(sits up suddenly, points to imaginary Ohio River down below)*. Lookit that!
DAVE. What?
BILL *(stands, steps forward, looking right)*. Barge!
TOM *(coming to stand by BILL, looking right)*. Three-wide!
DAVE *(coming to stand by TOM, looking left)*. Where?
BILL *(glances at DAVE)*. *Up* stream, Dave!
DAVE *(looks right)*. Oh. Oh golly.
TOM. Ya know what's great? When one's coming up stream and another's going down...
BILL *(pointing to imaginary point)*. ...and they meet right here at the horseshoe bend.
DAVE. Can't beat it.
TOM. Or how 'bout when they go through the locks?
BILL. Like old Dam 43?
DAVE. Wasn't that great?
TOM. Best damn lock on the Ohio River.
DAVE. Till they blew it up.
BILL. An engineering marvel.
DAVE. The lock or blowing it up?
BILL. The lock.
TOM. *That* would be the Panama Canal.
DAVE. Talking about your *locks*...

TOM. ...and Yankee know-how.

BILL. The men that died building that ditch.

DAVE. Mosquitoes, wasn't it?

TOM. I always wondered about that.

DAVE. 'bout what?

TOM. Think they all really died of yellow fever...

BILL. Well—

TOM. ...or was it simply too hot?

DAVE. Equator hot.

BILL. Now *that's* hot.

TOM. Damn hot. *(Pause.)* Did ya know Disney thought about putting a park here?

BILL. No way.

TOM. If I'm lying I'm dying.

DAVE. Here?

TOM *(makes sweep with arm)*. Look at it, for chrissakes.

BILL. Those cliffs.

DAVE *(points to the sky)*. Those hawks.

TOM *(points to the river)*. That water.

DAVE. Last thing we need is Mr. Frog's Wild Ride here in Leavenworth, Indiana.

BILL. *Toad's.*

DAVE. What?

BILL. Mr. *Toad's* Wild Ride, not Mr. *Frog's.*

DAVE. Whatever.

TOM. Who needs Disney?

BILL. Good riddance.

DAVE. But a restaurant...

TOM. ...with big plate windows—

BILL. *Now* you're talking. And *Italian.*

DAVE. With outside seating.
TOM. No way. Who wants to eat pasta in this heat...
BILL. ...this humidity?
TOM. Lookit that haze sittin' out there all fat and sassy.
BILL. Makes me sick just thinking about it.
DAVE. The haze?
BILL. The soggy pasta. *(They sit back down.)*
DAVE. 'Course, there is a remedy.
BILL. What?
DAVE. We could go in the house where it's air-conditioned. *(Long pause as they think it over.)*
BILL. Nah.
TOM. No way.
DAVE. We're all right.
TOM. Think I'll get that beer. *(He doesn't move. Lights fade.)*

END

TWILIGHT SERENADE
by
John Green

CHARACTERS

RUBY: In her 80s.

TOM: Her son-in-law, in his 40s.

YOUNG MAN: In his 20s.

PLACE: Various locations.

TIME: The present.

TWILIGHT SERENADE

AT RISE: *RUBY pulls a shopping list and coupons from her purse. TOM tries to be patient. They are in a drug store.*

RUBY *(reading from her list).* I need the Aleo... um, Al... green... it's... on sale, in a green bottle.
TOM *(takes the list).* Aleo...? Aloevera. Aloevera, Ruby. It's, um, right here. *(He takes a bottle off the rack.)* Here. *(He hands it to her. She puts it in her basket.)*
RUBY. Thank you. I get so forgetful. Thank you, Tom.
TOM. Sure.
RUBY *(reading from her list).* Cards. I need three birthday cards.
TOM. Three?
RUBY. Well, yes. There's Josephine and Jack and, um, oh damn...
TOM. You're doing fine.
RUBY. I can't remember...
TOM. Marcia?
RUBY. Marcia. Marcia. Oh, Lord.
TOM *(to audience).* I don't mind taking her shopping. Really. But the greeting cards. She reads them. Out loud! *(She takes greeting cards from a rack, carefully reading each one aloud.)*
RUBY. "Each season is unique and beautiful
    beyond expression, so too is every age

        To look with pride in every year
        to dream and plan anew... "
TOM. Slowly.
RUBY. "To treasure friendships you hold dear
        To think and hope and do... "
TOM. One-at-a-time.
RUBY *(reading the second card)*.
    "With special thoughts of you
    Thinking of you on your birthday
    Hoping that today brings you the best
    Wishing you much joy and happiness in the future
    Because you deserve nothing less... "
TOM. It's like Chinese water torture.
RUBY *(reading the third card)*.
    "A lifetime friend is one who shares
    both sad and happy days
    she shows how much she cares for you
    In many thoughtful ways
    A lifetime friend will stand by you
    whatever life may bring
    And having her to trust and turn to
    Means just everything... "
TOM. As if anybody cares what they say!! *(He looks at his watch.)*
RUBY. I'm sorry. Do you have an appointment?
TOM *(to her again)*. No. No no, take your time. It's fine.
RUBY. So many choices.
TOM. Let's see. *(He glances at the cards.)* This looks good. That's nice. These are fine.

RUBY. Okay. *(Starts to put them in her basket, stops.)* But Josephine just lost her husband. This might be too emotional. What do you think?

TOM *(reads it)*. "A lifetime friend is one who shares both sad and happy days..." Well, maybe you're right. Why don't you go ahead and look some more.

RUBY. You sure?

TOM. No problem. *(She does. He faces the audience and screams silently, regains his composure and turns back to her, tight smile.)* What else is on your list? *(She takes it out of her purse.)*

RUBY. Just the Tylenol.

TOM. I'll get it. *(He starts off.)*

RUBY. The caplets. Not the, um...

TOM. Gel tabs?

RUBY. They're too large for my throat. I have trouble swallowing them.

TOM. Right. *(Starts again.)*

RUBY. Regular. *(He stops.)* Not extra-strength. I'm sorry.

TOM. Regular. It's no problem, Ruby. Really. *(He exits. She faces audience.)*

RUBY *(with humor)*. Don't grow old—if you can avoid it. Oh, he tries so hard. I know he gets impatient. But he's a good man. My daughter's lucky. I just... I lost my David—my husband—two years ago today. I wish you had known him. He was handsome. Tall. Six feet, two inches exactly.

(A handsome YOUNG MAN enters, dressed in clothing from the 1940s.)

RUBY. I met him at Borden's. The dairy company? He was in sales. I worked the switchboard. All the girls had their eye on him. *(She turns and mimes working an old-fashioned switchboard. He approaches, tries to kiss her. She blushes, turns away. He exits. She turns to find him gone. Reluctantly, she picks up another greeting card, starts to read.)* "As days go by and we recall..." *(Sighs.)* Too sad. *(Blackout.)*

SCENE TWO

(RUBY and TOM are seated at a restaurant table eating Greek salads.)

TOM. No. No, it's on the tip of my tongue.
RUBY. It's not herring, is it?
TOM. I don't think so. *(Looks at salad.)* No. Herring's creamy. You know, with that white sauce?
RUBY. Of course. Of course. What am I thinking? *(She picks up an anchovy with her fork.)* But it is a fish...
TOM. Salty...
RUBY. Caviar?
TOM. Not in this place. *(They share a laugh.)*
RUBY. How's the search going?
TOM. Pardon?
RUBY. The job search.
TOM *(defensive)*. I'm trying.
RUBY. Oh, I know you are. It takes time.

TOM. I've got same good prospects. Nothing concrete. *(Chuckles.)* Nothing concrete.

RUBY. Is that a joke? I don't...

TOM. Concrete? You know, I'm a contractor so...

RUBY. Anchovies.

TOM. What?

RUBY. Anchovies. These are anchovies.

TOM. Right. Right. Of course. *(Announcer.)* And the winner is—Ruby Winchester from Chicago, Illinois! *(Looks around.)* Where's Ed McMahon when you need him?

RUBY. Ed McMahon?

TOM. The Publisher's Clearinghouse. You know, all those prize deals?

RUBY. Oh, yes. Yes, of course. *(Pause.)* Concrete. *(She eats in silence.)*

TOM *(to audience).* I really don't have anywhere I have to be. That's what bothers me. She's sweet. Couldn't be nicer. But I...I sit here thinking, "Why the hell do I have time to eat lunch with my mother-in-law? What the hell's wrong with me?" I'm looking for work. I really am. *(Back to her.)* Anchovies.

RUBY. Sometime I'd like to have ribs.

TOM. It's a Greek diner, I don't think...

RUBY. No. At Carson's. Carson's ribs.

TOM. Oh. Sure. They deliver.

RUBY. I don't think so. You have to pick them up.

TOM. I'm sure they deliver.

RUBY *(sudden emotion).* I know they don't. David and I used to order them to go.

TOM. That doesn't mean they don't deliver.

RUBY. That's true. *(Beat.)* But I know for a fact they don't deliver. *(She addresses the audience.)* I don't drive. I never learned. When Molly—that's my daughter—when she was six, a woman on Eighteenth Street had an accident. She ran a red light and crashed into a bus—head-on. Three children were killed. I decided I would never learn to drive.
TOM. I had a dream last night.
RUBY. You did.
TOM. Yes. Like a dream. It seemed more real, actually. More real than a dream.
RUBY. I had a dream about *Wheel Of Fortune.* I met Pat Sajak.
TOM. No kidding.
RUBY. He's from Chicago, you know. Seems like a nice young man. *(Beat.)* What was yours?
TOM *(careful).* Well, it was about David,
RUBY. Oh.
TOM. Is that okay? Do you want to? I don't need to.
RUBY. No. I'd like to.

(The YOUNG MAN enters.)

TOM. Well. Let's see. It was him. Like he was standing here in front of us. *(TOM watches him, entranced.)* Only he was young again. You know how dreams are. He was explaining what happened after he died. After, well, you know, after such a—difficult time.
RUBY *(quiet).* It was so difficult.
TOM. He said: "I was contained in a plastic form like a..."

TOM & YOUNG MAN *(simultaneously).* ...a rectangle. I was confused. For a long time. Then, slowly the walls evaporated. And I ran. Freeeeeeeeeeeeeeeeeeeee! *(The YOUNG MAN runs about the stage, enjoying his new-found body, telling his story. TOM and RUBY sit at the table.)*
YOUNG MAN. I was back in Shelbyville. *(Breathes the air.)* Southern Illinois. It was summer. I was a boy. Everything was new. And alive. Earth magic!! *(He reaches up and mimes grabbing an apple off a tree.)* Apples. *(He follows a butterfly.)* Butterflies. *(Tries to grab it and misses. He lies on his back, closing his eyes.)* Sunlight. *(TOM walks over to him and lies down, entering the dream. After a restful moment, the YOUNG MAN bolts upright.)* You hear that? *(TOM sits up.)*
TOM. What?
YOUNG MAN. That. *(An old-fashioned train whistle.)*
TOM *(sad).* Oh, I see.
YOUNG MAN. I wanted to make sure everything was okay. It seems okay.
TOM. I think it is, David. I'm doing the best I can. I get impatient. Selfish.
YOUNG MAN. You're doing fine. *(He stands, TOM does the same.)* Take care of things.
TOM. You look great. *(They start to hug, then shake hands instead. TOM sits at the table again.)*
YOUNG MAN *(to audience).* We met at Borden's. By the water cooler. *(The YOUNG MAN leads RUBY by the hand to an imaginary water cooler.)* She was the prettiest thing I'd ever seen. She wore a peach scarf. *(He takes a scarf out of his pocket and drapes it about her*

neck. She looks up shyly and adjusts it. He offers his hand.) I took her dancing. At the Aragon Ballroom. It was a perfect spring night. Lawrence Avenue. Nineteen forty-four. *(They dance.)* And we owned that dance floor. *(A romantic tune from the Big Band era plays. He dances her gracefully around the stage. The train whistle blows. They gaze into one another's eyes. One last look. He kisses her goodbye, gently removes the scarf from her neck, then exits. She looks after him longingly, then finally takes her place at the table again across from TOM.)*

TOM. He got on the train and waved goodbye. That was it. *(Pause.)* He seemed happy.

RUBY. He was a good dancer.

TOM. He was?

RUBY. Oh, yes. Wonderful. Taught me all the new steps. He'd even make up his own.

TOM. Sounds like him. Well, it was a nice dream. I miss him. *(Touches her hand.)*

RUBY. Me too. *(Pause, releasing hands.)* You know, you may be right.

TOM. How's that?

RUBY. About Carson's. They may deliver.

TOM. They might.

RUBY. It's just that we always drove there and got them. We took them home ourselves. But they might deliver.

TOM. Maybe we can go there sometime.

RUBY. That'd be nice. That would be very nice. *(The same romantic tune as earlier plays. They finish their salads as lights fade slowly to black.)*

END

BOOK KEEPING
by
Irl Mowery

For Sally Parrish,
who suggested that I dramatize my story,
"The Book Keeper," which appeared in
the Fall 1992 issue of *Concho River Review*.

The playwright wishes to acknowledge the role played by Edward Albee's Workshop at the University of Houston in the development of this script.

* * * *

Book Keeping was presented in December 1993 as a staged reading at Scriptwriters/Houston, directed by Pat Brown with the following cast: Robert Strane and Jean Proctor.

It was further produced by Love Creek Productions in January 1994 at the off-off-Broadway Nat Horne Theatre, directed by Howell Mayer with the following cast: J.D. Watson and Lori Kessler.

In June 1994, The Attic Theatre Ensemble on Theatre Row in Hollywood presented *Book Keeping* with the following players: Weston Nathanson and Wendy Worthington. The director was Richard Hochberg.

Book Keeping was awarded first prize in The Attic Theatre's 2nd Annual One-Act/New Directors Marathon in 1994.

In April 1995, *Book Keeping* was produced at Stages Theatre in Houston as part of Edward Albee's Workshop. It was sponsored by the University of Houston and directed by Robert Bullard with the following cast: David Parker and Bonnie Gallup.

BOOK KEEPING

CHARACTERS

EDWIN: Husband.
PHYLIS: His wife.

PLACE: In and around Houston.
TIME: From June of one year to June of the next.

SETTING: *The stage is bare, except for two or three pairs of lightweight, straight chairs. Side by side, the chairs can represent a church pew, the front seat of a car, folding chairs at graveside or a workbench. Facing one another, they can suggest a breakfast table between them. [Props, except Edwin's little book, may be pantomimed.]*

AT RISE: *EDWIN stands in a pool of light, wearing a dark suit, white shirt, conservative tie and gold wedding band.*

EDWIN *(referring to a small book in his hand)*. It's not a conspicuous thing. Just a sliver of a book. Thin. Vest-pocket size, if I wore a vest. Dark blue leather with pale blue pages. If my wife ever finds this little book, I'm in trouble. *(Slipping the book into his shirt pocket.)* I bought it in a narrow, glue-scented shop in Venice, one afternoon while Phylis was resting at the hotel and I was rambling on my own, so she doesn't even know I have it.

(PHYLIS appears in a pool of light in the breakfast-table area. She wears an expensive-looking matronly dress, a single strand of good pearls and a large diamond solitaire with her wedding ring.)

PHYLIS *(speaking into a phone)*. Evelyn? Phylis. Guess what I've just done— I've just called the invitation service and told them that Edwin and I accept with pleasure the kind invitation to your granddaughter's wedding—and the reception, of course. I'm so glad she's having it at the *old* country club. So much patina there. How many bridesmaids?

EDWIN. Not that Phylis snoops among my things. If she went into the den and rummaged through my desk—for a large paper clip or a small rubber band—she would probably toss the book aside. *(Taking out book and moving to his workshop area.)* Even if she opened it, she wouldn't be able to decipher its contents. She would head straight for my workshop, where I make all my own frames for my butterfly collection, and she would probably say something like this:

PHYLIS *(examining an imaginary little book, without moving)*. Edwin, what in heaven's name is this?

EDWIN. What?

PHYLIS. This little tiny book.

EDWIN. A thin, vest-pocket-size book? Dark blue leather with pale blue pages?

PHYLIS. You needn't describe it. I am not blind.

EDWIN. I bought it in Venice. In a narrow, glue-scented shop one afternoon while rambling on my own.

PHYLIS. I don't care where it came from. I want to know what's in it.

EDWIN. Oh, just a few...jottings.

PHYLIS. Women's first names? A different name on every page?

EDWIN *(paging through his little book)*. There are forty-eight pages. I had to count them because the book is full, and I must either start over, using the backs of the pages and putting everybody out of sequence, or get another book. Which would double my risk of discovery. *(Pocketing the book.)* Phylis would have no compunction, as I have shown you, about confronting me *if* she ever found my little book. Which, of course, she hasn't. I make no attempt to hide it. We've never had secrets from one another. *(Going to breakfast-table area.)* We didn't, that is, until she broke our unwritten agreement. You see, Phylis and I have always been inseparable. All our friends remark about how much we seem to enjoy one another's company. *(EDWIN sits and reads a newspaper.)*

PHYLIS *(into phone)*. Carlotta, I cannot begin to tell you how much Edwin and I enjoyed the concert. You and Roger have such marvelous seats! *(Listening.)* Next time Roger goes hunting, I could pick you up and we could go to the concert together. *(Listening.)* Aren't you sweet! That's what everybody says. *(Hanging up. To EDWIN.)* Carlotta wanted both of us to have their symphony tickets because we seem to enjoy one another's company so much. She wouldn't dream of separating us.

EDWIN. Carlotta is very observant.

PHYLIS. Carlotta's my very best friend. You and I are so inseparable, we're the envy of all my friends.

EDWIN. Your friends envy you because I don't go hunting with my friends and leave you at home alone.

PHYLIS. Roger and Carlotta have nothing in common. But you and I really do enjoy the same things. Antiquing...

EDWIN. Chamber music...

PHYLIS. Jellied consomme...

EDWIN. Backgammon...

PHYLIS. We love just being together.

EDWIN. I couldn't imagine being with anybody else.

PHYLIS. Neither could I. That's why I worry sometimes.

EDWIN. Worry. What about?

PHYLIS. About...if anything should ever happen to either of us.

EDWIN. It's certainly going to happen to *one* of us. Sooner or later.

PHYLIS. Most people have their children to console them.

EDWIN. Instead of children, we have a lot of freedom. To buy things for ourselves. Go on trips whenever we take a notion.

PHYLIS. I have nobody to leave my silver to.

EDWIN. That'll be my problem. If anything happens to you first.

PHYLIS. Oh, Edwin. I can't bear to even think about either one of us being left behind.

EDWIN *(resuming his reading)*. Then don't think about it.
PHYLIS. Wouldn't it be wonderful if both of us...could make our exit together?
EDWIN. Simultaneously?
PHYLIS. At the same identical time.
EDWIN. Neat. But highly unlikely.
PHYLIS. What if we met with some kind of calamity? Like a marvelous plane crash?
EDWIN. Fine for us. But what about the rest of the passengers?
PHYLIS. On the way home, of course. From a marvelous place we'd never been to before.
EDWIN. After a couple of drinks...
PHYLIS. After the movie, of course...
EDWIN *(rising and addressing the audience)*. Phylis and I convinced ourselves that miraculously, somehow, we were going to check out simultaneously. We began to count on it. When we took out flight insurance, for instance, we made it payable to our church, instead of one another. That was before I started keeping my little book. *(Going to chairs representing the front seat of a car and sitting on the driver's side.)* Before we went to the wedding where I saw the woman with Good Hair. *(PHYLIS takes her seat on the passenger's side.)* Phylis, which church?
PHYLIS. You never listen to anything I tell you.
EDWIN. Tell me again. Where is the wedding?
PHYLIS. All Saints, Edwin. *(They ride for a moment in silence.)*
EDWIN. Phylis, who's getting married?

PHYLIS *(after a look that says she's told him a dozen times)*. Evelyn's granddaughter, Edwin.

EDWIN. Big wedding?

PHYLIS. Twelve bridesmaids. Brass quintet.

EDWIN. Are we invited to the reception?

PHYLIS *(with another look)*. Edwin...

EDWIN. Okay okay. Where?

PHYLIS. Country club. *(Before he can ask another question.)* The *old* country club.

EDWIN *(after a pause)*. Good thing we didn't have any daughters.

PHYLIS. I would have liked to do one wedding before I died.

EDWIN. Think of the expense. *(Shuddering.)* Think of the son-in-law.

PHYLIS. We could have had a son. Rehearsal dinners aren't all that expensive.

EDWIN. I wouldn't have minded a daughter-in-law.

PHYLIS. Alice showed her daughter-in-law's sonogram at bridge last week. You could see its little penis quite plainly.

EDWIN *(wincing)*. What an invasion of privacy!

PHYLIS. She needn't have bothered with a sonogram. I could have told her it was going to be a boy. *(They are silent as EDWIN turns into the church parking lot.)*

EDWIN. They're going to get a lot of gifts. Look at all the cars.

PHYLIS. There's a space. There, Edwin!

EDWIN. I see it.

PHYLIS. Quick! Before that Jaguar gets it!

EDWIN. Phylis, I *see* it. *(While EDWIN parks, PHYLIS inspects her teeth in the mirror behind the sun visor on her side. EDWIN gets out, goes around the car and opens the door for her.)* How did you know?
PHYLIS. Know what?
EDWIN. That Whatsername's baby was a boy?
PHYLIS. I could tell.
EDWIN. How?
PHYLIS. I can just *tell*. The way Mother could. You know. *(PHYLIS goes to chairs representing a church pew.)*
EDWIN *(to audience)*. Do I know! The way Phylis's mother used to look at me, I felt like I had lipstick all over my chin.
PHYLIS *(looking around the church)*. I just knew she'd have candelabra and smilax. *(Entering a pew.)* You go ahead and take the aisle seat.
EDWIN *(sitting, under protest)*. The candles will drip on my good suit.
PHYLIS *(sitting next to him)*. Be still. And lower your voice.
EDWIN *(in a loud whisper)*. This smilax is tickling my ear.
PHYLIS *(in a loud whisper)*. Stop turning around. You can stand up and look when the bride comes in.
EDWIN *(looking across the aisle)*. Why is Adelaide sitting on the groom's side?
PHYLIS *(into EDWIN's ear)*. See that bald-headed man?
EDWIN. Sitting beside Adelaide?
PHYLIS. That's her new husband.
EDWIN. Must be a friend of the groom.
PHYLIS. She met him on a marvelous cruise. *(They smile guiltily and wave to Adelaide.)*

EDWIN *(looking in the other direction).* Who is that woman?

PHYLIS *(craning her neck in both directions).* Which one?

EDWIN. In the row ahead. Over there.

PHYLIS. Oh. That's Lola Something-or-other. I met her at a style show the other day.

EDWIN *(savoring the name).* Lola.

PHYLIS. Recently moved down from Kenilworth. Her husband was an insurance executive. Before he collapsed.

EDWIN. I bet he was jogging.

PHYLIS. Along the lakefront. Look, there's Carlotta. In her new wig.

EDWIN *(rising, to the audience).* Lola! *(Pause.)* Before bed that night, even though I had consumed a quantity of champagne at the reception—or perhaps because of that—I made my first entry. In the four-line format which became my standard. *(Referring to his book.)* Lola. Statuesque. Good Hair. Possible. *(PHYLIS has gone to the breakfast-table area.)* About my format: I never record anything but the Christian name, for obvious reasons. The second word conjures up my initial overall impression of the lady. The third word, the attribute that most attracted me, is frequently physical. The fourth word, the evaluation, is self-explanatory. The other two words are—Impossible, and Probable. *(Turning toward PHYLIS.)* Phylis abrogated our pact quite abruptly. After Carlotta's husband died—suddenly. As Carlotta is Phylis's very best friend, Roger's death came as quite a shock. *(PHYLIS sits frozen in shock, phone to her ear.)* I'll take it. *(Taking the phone from PHYLIS and listening.)* Uh huh. Uh huh. I'll tell her. *(EDWIN hangs up, then supports PHYLIS to chairs representing graveside at a cemetery, talking to her en route.)* Roger had a stroke in mid-afternoon, when the health club was deserted. The towel boy found Roger floating facedown in the spa. One hundred and eight degrees Fahrenheit.

PHYLIS. I'm going to sit under the canopy next to Carlotta. *(Sitting.)* Her family has dwindled so.

EDWIN *(to audience)*. At the cemetery, Phylis sat next to her very best friend with an arm around her shoulder. After the service... *(Helping PHYLIS up and heading for the car.)* ...as our rector led the sobbing widow to the limousine, Phylis and I threaded our way through the tombstones to our car. *(To PHYLIS as he helps her into the car.)* If Roger had to have a stroke, he was damned lucky to drown like that.

PHYLIS *(fighting back a sob)*. What a hideous thing to say.

EDWIN. Better than being sentenced to a wheelchair the rest of his days. One side of his face sagging down, one arm hanging useless. Carlotta having to do his zipper...and so forth. *(As PHYLIS sobs quietly, EDWIN gets into the car and drives away. To audience.)* Back on the freeway, Phylis repaired her makeup in the mirror on the flipside of the visor.

PHYLIS. Edwin, I'm going to make a list. Of the music I want at my service.

EDWIN. What for?

PHYLIS. You can put it in your safe deposit box, along with my will.

EDWIN. We've always agreed that funerals are for the living. But if you like, I'll make a list, too. For *your* safe deposit box.

PHYLIS. That won't be necessary. *(Dabbing her nose with the tip of her hanky.)* I've decided to precede you.

EDWIN *(to audience)*. I didn't respond. Phylis often makes statements which she later reinterprets—even rescinds. Not until we reached our driveway did I fully comprehend that she had enunciated a major change in policy. We were waiting for the overhead door to rise when she gripped my forearm and elaborated.

PHYLIS. Darling Edwin, is it clear that I am not to be left behind?

EDWIN. If that's what you want.

PHYLIS. Not under any circumstances.

EDWIN. Then I'd better start taking care of myself.

PHYLIS *(getting out of car and heading for breakfast table)*. Every conceivable precaution.

EDWIN *(getting out of car)*. I'll join a health club. Staying out of hot water, of course. *(Giving him a look, PHYLIS sits and picks up phone. To audience, as he goes toward PHYLIS.)* Phylis's and my relationship was not immediately affected by her unilateral decision. As for the hostesses of our acquaintance... *(Sitting across from PHYLIS, speaking to audience.)* Roger was not the first male to be removed from their midst. Compounding an already horrendous problem. Place cards.

PHYLIS *(into phone)*. You can't do boy-girl-boy-girl without inviting at least one man that nobody knows anything about. *(Listening.)* No, you can't invite that one without inviting his friend—or whatever you call him. *(Listening.)* What we really need is for somebody's wife to pass away. *(Listening.)* Didn't I tell you about Edwin? That darling man has agreed to let me go first!

EDWIN. Now, Phylis...

PHYLIS. Oh no. Not any time soon. I'll see you tomorrow at the beauty parlor. *(PHYLIS hangs up.)*

EDWIN. I wish you hadn't started telling everybody. Some of the husbands have begun calling me Methuselah. And Jackson...

PHYLIS. I cannot stand that Jackson. Divorcing poor dear Alice, and marrying that young...female.

EDWIN. Jackson congratulated me in the men's room at the tennis matches. On getting you to agree to die off.

PHYLIS. Congratulated?

EDWIN. "Take it from one who knows," he said, "better an expensive funeral than alimony *ad infinitum.*"

PHYLIS. Nobody has any respect for Jackson. He never would have made all that money without Alice's connections.

EDWIN *(rising, to audience)*. Despite Phylis's having gone public about our altered status, it didn't occur to me, at first, to wonder what life without her might be like. Then, *my* best friend, Hector, had his wife die on him. *(PHYLIS leads EDWIN toward cemetery chairs.)* An embolism, in the middle of the night.

PHYLIS *(seating EDWIN in funeral chair)*. For which, unlike you and I, Hector was totally unprepared.

EDWIN *(swiping his cheeks)*. What's the matter with me? I only cry at weddings.

PHYLIS *(her hand on his shoulder)*. Go ahead. Let it all out.

EDWIN. How is Hector going to get through the rest of this day?

PHYLIS. Edwin, it's time to lay your carnation on her coffin. *(Getting no response.)* Edwin...

EDWIN *(rising and disposing of the carnation)*. How will Hector get through tomorrow? And next week? All by himself?

PHYLIS *(leading EDWIN away)*. The first year will be the hardest. Her birthday. Then Christmas. Then their anniversary.

EDWIN *(to audience)*. I could tell that Phylis had given the matter some thought. *(PHYLIS returns to her phone. To audience.)* Phylis and her friends, wives and widows alike, gathered around and took care of Hector.

PHYLIS *(into phone)*. Precious, I think you should get your mother's things out of her bedroom, unobtrusively, as soon as possible. No no no—don't trouble your father with any details. Just give it all away. *(Listening.)* Well then, burn it.

EDWIN *(to audience)*. Following a highly developed procedure for handling the bereaved, in a surprisingly short time, the hostesses began including Hector in low-pressure social events.

PHYLIS *(into phone)*. Without being presumptuous, might I suggest including Hector? Such a gentle man. *(Listen-*

ing.) No no, I wouldn't pair him up with anybody. Yet. Leave him free to contribute as much—or as little—as he feels like.

EDWIN *(sitting across from her, to PHYLIS).* I seem to notice that whenever Hector is included, several widows or divorcees are always on hand.

PHYLIS. Darling Edwin, surely you must realize that Hector, after forty years of monogamy, is once again an eligible male.

EDWIN. What makes you think he's...ready?

PHYLIS. I can tell.

EDWIN. How?

PHYLIS. I can just tell.

EDWIN *(rising, to audience).* Sometimes I think Phylis is a mind reader. I had no idea how Hector felt about this ritual. I tried to place myself in his position, by pretending that Phylis had already...left me to my own devices. But I found it an impossible stretch of the imagination. Now, all the women in our set have been around long enough to know how to capitalize on their assets, physical and otherwise. But when I projected myself into the single state, confronted with the choice of either selecting a new mate or eking out my days on the stag line, I simply shriveled up.

PHYLIS *(into phone).* An extra man? What about Hector? He's back in circulation.

EDWIN *(to audience).* I simply could not visualize myself climbing into bed with the former wife of any man with whom I had ever played poker or watched football. Finally, I realized that—actuarially speaking—despite my belated exertions at the health club, the odds were that Phylis was going to outlive me. So...I decided to stop torturing myself with hypothetical choices.

PHYLIS *(into phone)*. No no. Don't seat him *next* to her; too obvious. Put him *across* from her—between two married women.

EDWIN *(to audience)*. Then, we happened to sit behind that attractive newcomer at that wedding. And completely without warning, I experienced the breakthrough that started me using my little blue book. *(Taking out the book.)* Lola. Statuesque. Good Hair. Possible. *(Pocketing the book.)* The attribute that most attracted me in this case was physical; the lady had naturally wavy hair, cut rather short. Emerging from a pool, she would have only to shake her head, run her fingers through her hair, and it would fall into place. Like a man's hair. I could imagine myself married to a woman with hair like that.

PHYLIS *(into phone)*. Hector hasn't invited you to his party? I'll remind him.

EDWIN *(taking out his book, to audience)*. Lola Something-or-other opened the gate upon a secret garden inhabited by women whose husbands I had never met. Do not assume, however, that I binged on an abundance of females who, being unattached, might become potential partners. On the contrary, I have been quite abstemious.

PHYLIS *(into phone)*. If you haven't decided which cruise to take, I understand that Hector's doing the Inside Passage.

EDWIN *(to audience)*. I do not leaf through my book, fantasizing over the contents. It is strictly an *aide-memoire*.

To be referred to only when, and if, the melancholy necessity should arise. *(Riffling the pages of his book.)* It has taken me over a year to make the forty-eight entries that bring me now to the final page. And to a momentous decision: whether to start another book. *(Pocketing the book and sitting opposite PHYLIS.)* Then, during this morning's breakfast conversation, Phylis made a startling revelation.

PHYLIS *(to EDWIN)*. Have you spoken with Hector lately?

EDWIN *(to PHYLIS)*. Hector's on a cruise.

PHYLIS. He's back. Didn't he tell you?

EDWIN. Tell me what?

PHYLIS. He's getting married.

EDWIN. Hector? Who's he marrying?

PHYLIS. Lola Davenport.

EDWIN. Lola who?

PHYLIS. You know. Lola. The one with Good Hair.

EDWIN *(rising, to audience)*. Any observations I make in the future will be strictly mental. There's really no need to commit them to paper. I have a phenomenal memory.

END

THERE WAS A BIGNESS
by
Erik Ramsey

CHARACTERS

CHARLIE SPOON: A very functional alcoholic, 70.

LARRY: A young liquor clerk, 22.

PLACE: The small town of Thermopolis, Wyoming.

TIME: The year is 1991.

THERE WAS A BIGNESS

SETTING: *Late at night in a tiny package liquor store. Shelves of bottles tower over an old cash register. Neon beer signs hang in a window covered with faded sale posters.*

AT RISE: *LARRY is dusting shelves and liquor bottles with a wet rag. We hear a toilet flush and SPOON enters from the rear of the store positioning his suspenders and donning a long winter jacket.*

SPOON. You could tell outta the gate that boy was a ticker-tape time bomb.
LARRY *(continues to dust as he converses)*. Say again?
SPOON. Ticker-tape time bomb. I could see it coming. Like that Dan Clyburg piano guy.
LARRY. Uh... Paddle back a bit.
SPOON. That Buster Douglas fella. Good name for a fighter. Boy had a fine hook. No jab though. It's all jab now, even with the big boys.
LARRY. No, I meant about the time bomb.
SPOON. What about it?
LARRY. What'd you call it?
SPOON. What? A ticker-tape time bomb?
LARRY. Yeah.
SPOON. So?
LARRY. What's it mean exactly?

SPOON. Oh hell. Say a guy wants to be a ball player... shit... No, say a guy wants to be a doctor... Well, it's like counting calves before the bull ejaculates. Like swingin' the bat before the ball is even pitched.

LARRY. Uh... Nope. Keep going.

SPOON. Damn... Okay-okay-okay-okay! You remember Nate Jellybean?

LARRY. Jellybean?

SPOON. Jellybean ain't his real name. *(SPOON slips a pint of gin from a shelf into his pocket. LARRY doesn't notice, still intent on his dusting.)* It's, uh, like Jostlebyne, or Jastlebann.

LARRY. Still don't know him. Never followed the sport too close.

SPOON. I wondered about that some.

LARRY. I'm not a clown.

SPOON. You'd make a good one though. I seen it in your genes.

LARRY. You were telling me about a jellybean time bomb.

SPOON. Nate Jellybean. He wasn't no great bull rider, but he had his spells. We all got our spells, you know. Anyway, picture this: State Fair in '58. Second or third year in the Douglas Fairgrounds, which was brand new then. Long, fresh white paint in the stands. Full of red and blue ribbon. See it? Nate was from Douglas, raised up near there, and them new fairgrounds inspired the spell in him. Get this—he rode Pudding! *(SPOON flourishes to emphasize his awe.)*

LARRY. So?

SPOON *(flourishes again)*. Pudding! I remember 'cause I was in the barrel for him. And them barrels wasn't those padded deals you got today. They was real drums. Some still had linseed in 'em that year because I got a rash that couldn't be explained by any old bed-sheet or toilet-seat story.

LARRY. Pudding was a mean bull?

SPOON. See? I knew you remembered.

LARRY. I don't think I was born yet.

SPOON. Doesn't matter, point is... point is...

LARRY. Tickertape Nate and his spell.

SPOON. Exactly. Exactly. Nate beat Pudding. He had his one and only spell and rode the foulest bull in the region. Pudding was whipped only once before. Of course Nate took the state in '58. *(SPOON slips a pint of whiskey into his other jacket pocket. This time LARRY sees him do it out of the corner of his eye, but continues to dust.)* But he couldn't stand the pressure of everybody following his ride. Fell down flat at Frontier Days. Never rang the bell again.

LARRY. How's that a time bomb?

SPOON. One parade and old Nate was all bound up. The brass bands hog-tied his hands. He was jaundiced by the bite of the glory bug and the spell was broken.

LARRY *(laughing)*. I got you, I got you. Ticker-tape time bomb. I'll remember that.

SPOON. Shit... Your daddy never told you that?

LARRY. Dad's dead.

SPOON. Dang, Larry.

LARRY. Forget it. Over a year now.

SPOON. I do apologize. I get around so much that I see and hear a speck of each and a whole truck of nothing.

LARRY. He went like he wanted.

SPOON. Good. That's good... He was a solid man. A real fine solid Joe. I remember when he was knee high to a— *(LARRY cuts him off, abruptly stopping dusting.)*

LARRY. He was an asshole and you know it.

SPOON. Yep. Sure enough.

LARRY. Didn't he beat the crap out of you once?

SPOON. Probably a couple of times for all I can recollect. The man didn't mix well with liquor. He was a fine clown though. Saved thousands of ranch boys from growing extra or'fices.

LARRY. Didn't he also call you a sage-nigger?

SPOON. No, he never.

LARRY. I heard him call you that.

SPOON. No. See, it wasn't like that though.

LARRY. How could you just stand there and take his crap?

SPOON. You were too young to know the other steeps of it.

LARRY. You poor ignoramus.

SPOON. I know how it was meant.

LARRY. They kicked you like a dog.

SPOON. I had sharp teeth.

LARRY. Sharp teeth. You licked their hands for the trouble.

SPOON. You remind me of him a touch.

LARRY *(suddenly grabs SPOON by the lapels)*. Don't you ever!

SPOON. Easy boy, easy. Don't go proving my point for me.

LARRY *(lets go of SPOON and returns to his dust rag).* Son of a bitch. It's just being stuck in this pickled place. When I left I thought I'd never come back. But there was always something about this town. There was a bigness... And not what the idiot tourists think about us either. Not just cowboy hats.

SPOON *(slips a pint of vodka into his pants. LARRY sees him do it, but SPOON doesn't see LARRY watching).* I went to Mel's funeral in a Cadillac. But you got it wrong. It ain't "where," son. It's "how."

LARRY. I'm not sure I can swallow any more medicine tonight, Mr. Spoon.

SPOON. Tell me: Why are you here?

LARRY. I told you. Dad died.

SPOON. So?

LARRY. So somebody had to take over the store.

SPOON. Why not somebody else?

LARRY. There isn't anybody else. Look, I ran this store even before I left for school. I did everything but sell the liquor. I did the stock and balanced the books. And then after I went to the university, I came back and busted ass in the summer to build it up from what Dad did to it while I was away.

SPOON. Your daddy had some good pieces in his puzzle too.

LARRY. You wouldn't even be talking to me if you didn't need some firewater, chief.

SPOON. Maybe so. It don't matter. It just seems to me you're taking it by the horns rather than dancing it down the exit chute and loading up for another. *(Pause.)* What'd you learn in school?

LARRY *(sarcastic)*. That spelling counts.

SPOON. Yeah? Congratulations.

LARRY. Fuck. I'm a ticker-tape time bomb. For all this, I have a degree in literature.

SPOON. Don't mind me, I'm just an old sage-nigger. *(He winks.)* Actually, I'm only half injun. My ma was Scotch.

LARRY. I'm sorry I huffed at you, Mr. Spoon.

SPOON. Hell, son, I rattle off remedies faster than a sweaty shaman. *(A bottle hidden and lodged in SPOON's pants drops obviously to the floor, but does not break. Both men look each other in the eye for a beat. SPOON backs up slightly.)* But I make a better clown. That's where the money was, for me anyway. Your daddy and his friends—they kept me around for entertainment. I know that. But I also know that the old medicine men dressed up like clowns sometimes to heal their people. You ever hear of that? The whole idea of clowns was invented by Indian healers! Can you believe that, Larry? Can you?

LARRY *(stoops and slowly retrieves the bottle, placing it back on the shelf)*. Sure enough, Mr. Spoon.

SPOON. Them old-time healers was really something. I see what you were saying about bigness.

LARRY. How are you fixed these days?

SPOON. Fair enough. Room and board. Alan Fremont has me watching his calves.

LARRY *(moving behind the register)*. The usual tonight?

SPOON. How about Beam instead. I feel I need a step up.

LARRY *(takes down a half-pint from the shelves behind the register and rings it up)*. Two and fifteen.

SPOON. There's three and keep it.

LARRY. Thank ya, sir.

SPOON. Sure enough. You're a fine man, Larry... There's only one solution when you bite off more than you can chew: drop some back on your plate and keep chewing the rest.

LARRY. Yeah, sure, but how do you know which to spit and which to chew?

SPOON. Which isn't going to break your teeth? *(He turns to exit, his pockets bulging, and forgets the half-pint he paid for.)*

LARRY. Uh, Mr. Spoon? You forgot your bottle.

SPOON *(turns back and retrieves the bottle).* Call me Charlie, son. *(Again turns to exit.)*

LARRY. Charlie?

SPOON *(stops. Doesn't look at LARRY).* Yeah.

LARRY. Uh... Nothing. Good night, Charlie.

SPOON. Sure enough. *(SPOON exits. Lights out.)*

END

PUT YOUR BEST
FOOT FORWARD
by
Kent R. Brown

CHARACTERS

MOTHER
CLEANING LADY

PLACE: Backstage at a beauty pageant.

TIME: The present.

PUT YOUR BEST FOOT FORWARD

AT RISE: *Lights fade up on the MOTHER and the CLEANING LADY. The CLEANING LADY is dusting. The MOTHER is opening up a series of shoe boxes. Several pairs of high-heeled shoes are already on the floor.*

MOTHER. This pair, aren't they beautiful? Birmingham, Alabama. Cheryl Mae Sue, poor dear, she'd broken the heel on a lovely pair her grandma Abbott bought her for the little romp we had in Tallahassee. She couldn't walk around barefooted, could she?

CLEANING LADY. Sure couldn't. Guess not.

MOTHER. So there I was, from store to store. Not the right size, or too high. It was awful.

CLEANING LADY. I can imagine.

MOTHER. Finally...

CLEANING LADY. You found it, right?

MOTHER. The sweetest little bald man you ever did see. Had 'em right there. Tipped the cab boy twenty dollars to run two lights.

CLEANING LADY. What else could you do?

MOTHER. Took third place!

CLEANING LADY. Well, that's a start.

MOTHER. And these here...when Cheryl Mae Sue and I were in Slidell, Mississippi...rained!! Lord, did it rain.

CLEANING LADY. First place?

MOTHER. Slipped and fell...and chipped her tooth...

CLEANING LADY. That'll happen.
MOTHER. Got the Good Scout award though...for being such a trooper.
CLEANING LADY. That's something anyway.
MOTHER. These here are from Beaumont, Texas. Fifth place. And these, see how they shine? Got second place in Neosho, Missouri, the Little Miss Mo pageant.
CLEANING LADY. Moving up the line.
MOTHER. Oh, my, yes, and these shoes helped us all the way. I call them Lucky Shoes. Gotta put your best foot forward. *(Sings.)*
> Put your best foot forward
> It's a brand new day.
> Somethin' wonderful's gonna happen
> Things are goin' your way.
> When ya put your best foot forward
> That's what I always...say!

CLEANING LADY. Catchy tune. You make that up?
MOTHER. Cheryl Mae Sue's grandma did. Grandma Abbott, on her daddy's side. Sang her that song when she bought Cheryl Mae Sue her first pair of shoes. Bobby Clyde, that's Cheryl Mae Sue's daddy, Bobby Clyde and me didn't make too many ends meet in those days.
CLEANING LADY. Well, that's what family's for. To help out.
MOTHER. Go ahead.
CLEANING LADY. Go ahead?
MOTHER. Put 'em on.
CLEANING LADY. Put on those shoes?
MOTHER. Go on, any pair you like. Those blue ones got us fourth place in the Miss Bathhouse contest in Hot

Springs, Arkansas. Try the red ones if you want. They're the prettiest.

CLEANING LADY. They're real nice.

MOTHER. They are, aren't they?

CLEANING LADY. First place?

MOTHER. Almost. Cheryl Mae Sue dropped her baton... bounced right out into the judges' row. Poor thing, her face was as red as her shoes. But she walked right to the edge of the stage and smiled real nice and held out her hand. The judge gave it back to her and everybody applauded. People are real nice. They know it's a lot of work to keep from looking scared. Go ahead. Try 'em on.

CLEANING LADY (*sitting down and trying on the pair of red shoes*). Bet they won't fit. Don't look at my runs. Can't keep a decent pair of hose in this job.

MOTHER. I know. Used to waitress at this pancake place outside of Macon... on your feet all day.

CLEANING LADY. It's a killer. Oh, look. They fit.

MOTHER. Go ahead, walk around. They make you feel real good, don't they? (*The CLEANING LADY stands up cautiously and then, as she feels more confident, begins to walk like a beauty contestant.*) Perfect. Head up just a little bit. There... now... the turn... good, step, pivot! Back straight! Perfect!

CLEANING LADY. Makes ya feel like a...

MOTHER. Winner?

CLEANING LADY. Yeah. Like a winner.

MOTHER. "And now... the next Ms. ..."

CLEANING LADY. Mrs.

MOTHER. "... Mrs. Wonderful is..."

CLEANING LADY. Lolabelle Jenks! *(The MOTHER applauds as the CLEANING LADY bows and waves to her "subjects.")* I won. I'm Mrs. Wonderful!

MOTHER. Wasn't that fun?

CLEANING LADY. Mrs. Wonderful. Imagine that. After all these years someone finally recognizes I'm wonderful. *(Begins to take the shoes off.)* Well, break time's over. Back to work. *(Puts on her working shoes. The MOTHER begins to pack up the shoes.)* Thanks. Which pair is Cheryl Mae Sue gonna wear this time?

MOTHER. Don't know yet. Maybe I'll get her a new pair.

CLEANING LADY. It's gonna cost ya some red-light money.

MOTHER *(preparing to leave).* Well, if it takes every dime I've got, Cheryl Mae Sue's gonna have the prettiest shoes money can buy.

CLEANING LADY. Tell her "good luck" for me.

MOTHER. Hope ya didn't mind me showin' you the shoes. Helps get over my nerves. Nothing much to do but sit around and wait.

CLEANING LADY. Anytime. And thanks. Felt like Cinderella.

MOTHER. Ya looked great. *(The MOTHER exits. The CLEANING LADY returns to her work.)*

CLEANING LADY. Mrs. Wonderful. Finally. *(Sings.)*
    Put your best foot forward...
    It's a...nice...new day
    Somethin' wonderful's happenin'
    Get outta my way...
    When ya put two feet forward
    That's what I always...say!
Yeah! *(Blackout.)*

END

A LITTLE SUPPORT
by
L.B. Hamilton

CHARACTERS

LILY: Attractive, 55 to 60.

MEHTA: Lily's slightly younger sister.

PLACE: The kitchen of Lily's Brooklyn apartment.

TIME: A Saturday morning. The present.

A LITTLE SUPPORT

AT RISE: *MEHTA, who wears a plain comfortable running suit, sits at LILY's kitchen table and sips coffee as LILY, maybe just a bit nervous this morning, busies herself at the counter. LILY is dressed more formally than her sister, and has freshly coifed, newly dyed red hair.*

MEHTA. So to what do I owe this pleasure? We haven't had coffee together since you got the job. *(Looking around.)* Where's Sam?

LILY. I thought we could just talk alone for once. Drink. *(Indicating coffee.)* I put cinnamon in, just the way you like.

MEHTA. You're lookin' younger, Lily. New hair, new clothes—pretty classy. Workin' must be good for you.

LILY. Well, it's good for now. I never pictured myself serving up deli plates at this age. *(Pause.)* So what are you up to tonight, Mehta?

MEHTA. Up to? What would I be up to? I'll walk my poodle, then tune in Turner for a while.

LILY. Have a cookie. *(Pause.)* You shouldn't have to spend a Saturday like that, hunh?

MEHTA. Tell me. How much weight have you lost anyway? Sam must be thinkin' he has a new woman around.

LILY. So, you don't have plans tonight, hunh? Maybe you could stop by, or something?

MEHTA. I'm here already. Would you stop flittin' around? Now, what are we talkin' about?

LILY. Eat! They'll just go to waste. *(Pause.)* Mehta? Maybe you'd like to do me a little favor.

MEHTA. So, this isn't about us havin' a sisterly visit after all. Humph. I shoulda known.

LILY. Don't be like that. I just thought maybe you could baby-sit for me tonight.

MEHTA. Oh, sure... what? Wait a minute, you don't got any little kids.

LILY. There's Sammy. You always said Sam's a baby. Try this, it's got macadamias in it.

MEHTA. You want I should baby-sit Sam?

LILY. Kinda. *(Forcing the cookies.)* Here.

MEHTA. Stop with the cookies, already. Some of that dye get into your brain, Lily?

LILY. You don't have to do much. Just—like, invite him somewhere. You can invite your brother-in-law somewhere, right?

MEHTA. You want maybe I should take him to the zoo and buy him a balloon, or something?

LILY. Oh, stop. *(Pause.)* Maybe dinner. Dinner would be nice, hunh?

MEHTA. And where would you be?

LILY. Some friends at the deli want to go bowling. You know Sam hates bowling. *(Pause.)*

MEHTA. Ahhh. I get it. Sam's pullin' an attitude over you havin' a job.

LILY. It's not that.

MEHTA. Well you know what? Fuck him.

LILY. Mehta!

MEHTA. It's a old story. Someone's happy—he's sulking. Fuck him. Give me a cookie.

LILY. He just gets lonely. It happens.

MEHTA. Yeah? We all get lonely. Don't he think I know lonely?

LILY. Yeah... People get lonely.

MEHTA. Actin' like there's only room for one person to be happy in every relationship. What makes him so special, hunh?

LILY. Mehta, there's this...

MEHTA. You just make him go bowling. That's all. *(Pause.)* Sam like the hair?

LILY. Who knows? I came home from the shop and he just stared at me and asked if we were having fish for dinner. *(Pause.)* Mehta, I want...

MEHTA. You think that color would look good on me? I feel like I'm gettin' ready for a change.

LILY. No. You're a winter type. Winter types can't do the reds.

MEHTA. Winter type, hunh? *(Pause.)* So? Sam like the new you? *(Pause.)*

LILY. Sure. Want a cookie?

MEHTA. What's that?

LILY. Chocolate chip.

MEHTA. No, not that. The pause.

LILY. What pause?

MEHTA. Right before "sure." That pause.

LILY. I... Nothing. Look, I got myself acrylics to go with the hair. You should get some. It'd give you a lift.

MEHTA. Pah. What's an old lady need with acrylics? They are nice though.

LILY. It'd give you a lift.

MEHTA. You know, Lily? I think I should get me a job again. Something new.

LILY. You don't need a job. You just need some fun. Maybe you and Sam could go to the Mezmer tonight—they have music and dancing.

MEHTA. That's it! What the hell are you up to, Lily? You think I should take Sam dancing?

LILY. I told you I've got something to do... and, well, it would just be better if Sam could be busy and all.

MEHTA. No. Unhunh, I know you, Lily, you act real busy when you're hiding something... *(She considers LILY, then gasps.)* Ohmygod, you got a man!

LILY. Now, Mehta.

MEHTA. You got a man and you want me to cover for you! That's what this is all about! I don't hear from you for weeks, then all of a sudden, I'm useful.

LILY. No, Mehta! He's just a friend. I just want to go bowling with one of my new friends.

MEHTA. Go on! A friend you invite to dinner and introduce to people. You don't ask your sister to... You crazy? You're an old lady. You're gonna start sneaking around? You nuts?

LILY. Okay! Okay. Forget it.

MEHTA. A friend. Humph. Who do you think you're talking to?

LILY. Okay! *(They sip coffee in silence.)* Maybe he wants to be just a little more than a friend.

MEHTA. Hah! Didn't I know? Didn't I say that?
LILY. Oh stop. Nothing's happened.
MEHTA. You think I'm stupid? Trying to play Miss Innocent with me. I'm your sister.
LILY. I know. I know. *(Pause.)* Mehta? I need an adventure.
MEHTA. Adventure! You're talkin' about adultery. That's a pretty big adventure. You wanna kill Sam, or something? You wanna give him a heart attack?
LILY. That's where you come in. You said yourself, you're lonely.
MEHTA. I did not. When did I say I was lonely?
LILY. You did. What am I asking you? A little support, that's all. You'd rather watch colorized movies?
MEHTA. I think you shoulda left that hair alone, Lily, it's gone to your head.
LILY. Very funny. What's the matter with me having some fun, hunh? You've been divorced thirty years now.
MEHTA. So what?
LILY. So I watched you go out and have fun. You even went to Europe—two times! What did I do? I watched Sam feed his face.
MEHTA. At least you got someone who's comin' home for dinner. Me? I water my plants, then I talk to my poodle, then... then I talk to my plants.
LILY. You should be happy they don't pout when you come home.
MEHTA. Spare me the misery, Lily. Look at you. You got everything you always said you wanted and now you're

bitchin'. Me? I got a '88 Chrysler and a retirement check. Do you hear me bitchin'?

LILY. So, if life's so bad, you could use an adventure, too. Right?

MEHTA. An adventure with my sister's husband? Give me a break.

LILY *(pause, then calmly).* Just where do you get off being so damned righteous?

MEHTA. Righteous? What does that mean? You're goin' over the edge here, Lily.

LILY. You're talkin' like you never had an adventure with your sister's husband.

MEHTA. You know. Maybe you shouldn't have went to work. It's makin' you nervous. You got any more coffee? This is cold.

LILY. No. *(Pause.)* Well? *(Pause.)*

MEHTA. Well, what?

LILY. I said, you talk like you never had an adventure with your sister's husband. *(Pause.)* You hear me, Mehta?

MEHTA. I hear you. You're making me crazy with all this. I should go home.

LILY. Sit. Sit! *(MEHTA does. A thoughtful moment, then.)* You know what's funny, Mehta?

MEHTA. What?

LILY. You were always the smart one—the one who could handle everything. Yet you were so careless when you were with my Sammy.

MEHTA. What's that supposed to mean?

LILY. Tweed.

MEHTA. Tweed?

LILY. Tweed. It was your favorite perfume for years. You always poured it all over yourself. Used to make me sneeze, remember?

MEHTA. Yeah? So?

LILY. So, everytime Sam came home from you? I sneezed. *(Pause.)* What happened, anyway?

MEHTA. Happened?

LILY. One day, just like that, I stopped sneezing and Sam stopped playing tennis twice a week. *(No response.)* Oh stop with the guilty looks. *(Pause.)* So, did you enjoy it? I know Sammy perked up for a while there. Did you have fun, too? I mean when you weren't feeling so guilty and all.

MEHTA. I don't wan... Yes.

LILY. Good. That's good. So you didn't fight or anything when you broke up?

MEHTA. No, we just... Lily, I'm sorry.

LILY. No. That's good. No fight is good. That makes this all easier.

MEHTA. What. Oh no... Lily, we gotta calm down here and think straight, okay? Listen, we were all goin' through rough times, remember? Sam and me, we...

LILY. Did I ask for an explanation? I didn't ask for an explanation.

MEHTA. Damn it, Lily! I'm not going to seduce your husband!

LILY. You already did.

MEHTA. How do you know that, hunh? How do you know it was me? What if it was him?

LILY. Whatever. You owe me, Mehta.

MEHTA. It was a long time ago. It's different now.
LILY. Because I know? I always knew. You owe me, Mehta, and I'm collecting.
MEHTA. You're crazy. You know that?
LILY. Runs in the family. Look, just keep my husband busy when I want him busy. Damn it, Mehta, you said yourself, Sam's needy. I go to work, come home and he's mopin' around, waiting for me—watchin' me. I'm supposed to sit with him and stare at CNN. A big night is renting videos. No, uhn hunh... you listen to me... *I need an adventure and I'm going to have me one.* (*Pause.*) So who's getting hurt, hunh?
MEHTA. Why do I get the funny feeling it's gonna be me?
LILY. Good, then I won't have to put up with your phony guilt.
MEHTA. Lily... Sam hasn't looked at me in years.
LILY. Then you'll make him look at you. You'd rather spend Saturday night with a poodle? (*She goes to her purse and pulls out a business card.*)
MEHTA. Yeah! (*Pause.*) Yeah. Maybe.
LILY. You tell Sam you need to move your sofa or something. Get him to talk a little, bring up old times. Then... who knows? (*LILY offers MEHTA the card.*)
MEHTA. What's this?
LILY. My hairdresser's address. You have a one o'clock appointment. Tell her you need to look gorgeous for tonight.
MEHTA. You actually made an appointment for me? You are crazy. (*MEHTA looks steadily at LILY and does not*

take the card. LILY places the card on the table then goes to retrieve the cookie plate.)

LILY. Yeah. Nails too. You'll love it. Ask for Myrna.

MEHTA. I don't have to do this.

LILY. Let me get some more cookies. I got the kind with the sprinkles.

MEHTA. You can't make me do this, you know.

LILY. Oh relax, Mehta. I'm thinkin' this will probably all just fizzle out, then you'll be off the hook. After all, it'll probably take more than a new hair-do and some plastic fingernails for you to perk ole Sammy up. *(LILY places the cookie plate in front of MEHTA and smiles.)* You have kind of let yourself go and all, you know. *(LILY then turns to get the coffee pot, MEHTA stares at LILY's back, then picks up the business card, studies it.)*

MEHTA. So, Lily?

LILY. Yeah, Mehta?

MEHTA. So what kinda color is good for winter types? *(Lights fade to black.)*

END

RIDE OF A LIFETIME
by
David Alex

CHARACTERS

WIFE: Elderly, preferably in her 80s, still has plenty of spunk left in her.

HUSBAND: Elderly, in his 80s (90 would be nice). Every movement is an effort, but he still has a twinkle in his eye.

PLACE: The memory.

TIME: The present.

RIDE OF A LIFETIME

SETTING: *Two old wooden folding chairs.*

AT RISE: *WIFE and HUSBAND are sitting on chairs facing the audience. The actors never leave the chairs while on the "journeys" they take to overcome loneliness and boredom as well as the disappointment that their son never calls.*

HUSBAND occasionally raises his hands as though driving a car but soon returns them to his lap. Between their silences in the car, they encounter stops, turns and other traffic. As they transition into the "roller coaster" memory, they truly are taking the ride of a lifetime.

HUSBAND. You just went.
WIFE. You don't understand.
HUSBAND. You'll have to hold it in.
WIFE. You hold it.
HUSBAND. Don't make me laugh.
WIFE. What?
HUSBAND. I can hardly hold my own in, and you want me to hold yours.
WIFE. What are you going to do when you get older?
HUSBAND. If I get much older, I'll be younger.
WIFE. I remember one time you couldn't hold it in.
HUSBAND. Never.

WIFE. It was the last curve. Your hands were waving in the air like old glory reaching for who knows what.

HUSBAND. That's what you're supposed to do.

WIFE. You should have been down on the ground holding on to me.

HUSBAND. It was a glorious ride. With every part of my body shaking and vibrating on those wooden tracks, I'm surprised I had any insides left. Yep, they don't make 'em like they used to.

WIFE. They don't make anything like they used to.

HUSBAND *(goes to put his arm around her)*. That's for sure.

WIFE. ...LOOK OUT!

HUSBAND. What? What?

WIFE. Good Lord, are you trying to get us killed? You almost went off the road into those trees.

HUSBAND. I am in perfect control.

WIFE. Keep both hands on the wheel.

HUSBAND *(presses his foot as though accelerating while keeping both hands in his lap)*. I drive just as good with one. In fact, let's pick it up a little.

WIFE. Barney Oldfield you're not.

HUSBAND. My mother told me I could be whatever I want.

WIFE. I don't remember hearing her saying that.

HUSBAND. It was before I got married.

WIFE. I'm your mother now. Keep both hands on the wheel—and slow down.

HUSBAND. There... Feel better now?

WIFE. A man your age—

HUSBAND. —is still a man.

WIFE. I suppose.

HUSBAND. Suppose! I've got a mind to pull over and take you in the back seat.

WIFE *(laughs)*. It takes more than mind. *(Grimaces.)*

HUSBAND. What's the matter?

WIFE. I can't hold it in much longer.

HUSBAND. It's not safe to stand up in a moving vehicle. Now sit down, you'll ruin everything... Please.

WIFE. I'll try—but you better hurry.

HUSBAND. Think about something else.

WIFE. What do you mean?

HUSBAND. If you think about something else, it will take your mind off your problem.

WIFE. I don't have a problem. I just have to go to the toilet. *(She acts as though she is looking in the rearview mirror.)* You better stay to the right so that truck can pass us.

HUSBAND. What truck?

WIFE. The one getting ready to run us over. See? ...You spend too much time looking up the road. If you're going to drive, you have to know what's behind you.

HUSBAND. We're going forward not backward... You want to try it for a while?

WIFE. My reflexes aren't what they used to be.

HUSBAND. My pancreas isn't what it used to be.

WIFE. Pancreas?

HUSBAND. Yes.

WIFE. What does your pancreas do?

HUSBAND. I don't feel it doing anything. That's my point.
WIFE. ...Did anybody call today?
HUSBAND. A wrong number.
WIFE. What did they want?
HUSBAND. They were calling a restaurant—a Chinese one.
WIFE. I miss Chinese.
HUSBAND. If I see one, I'll pull over.
WIFE. Thank you. *(Silence.)*
HUSBAND. ...How often did *you* call your mother?
WIFE. Hardly ever.
HUSBAND. And your grandmother?
WIFE. Never.
HUSBAND. See.
WIFE. Who could afford a phone?
HUSBAND. If you had one—
WIFE. If I had one, I would have called them every day.
HUSBAND. Every day. What would you say?
WIFE. Hello. How are you? Did it rain today? I miss you. How's Dad? How's Granddad?
HUSBAND. You'd ask that every day?
WIFE. Yes.
HUSBAND. It would get boring.
WIFE. Words get boring. Love doesn't. *(Uncomfortable silence.)* So why doesn't anyone call?
HUSBAND. I don't know. *(He puts his arms around her.)* Maybe we should open our own Chinese restaurant. At least we'd hear from someone.

WIFE *(laughs lovingly, then).* Your hands—they're supposed to be on the wheel—like this.

HUSBAND. They get too tired if I hold them up so long.

WIFE. Your hands are supposed to be on the wheel.

HUSBAND. They get too tired when I hold them that way!

WIFE. Then don't make those phone calls. *(HUSBAND is preparing for a ride on a roller coaster. He eventually waves his hands in the air, etc.)* ...No, not there—stop! ...You know I'm afraid of heights.

HUSBAND. Just close your eyes and hold on to me... Going up is slow, but—raise your hands. Come on now. Higher.

WIFE. This one doesn't go upside down, does it? *(He holds one of her outstretched hands. They go on a wild roller coaster ride. He is having the time of his life. She is frightened at first.)* I won't go upside down. I won't go— ...oh...oh...oh...ooohhh! *(The ride is over.)*

HUSBAND. See, that wasn't so bad.

WIFE. ...Can we go again?

HUSBAND. Do you need to—you know—make your call first?

WIFE. It's too late... You're right. The last curve emptied me—pancreas and all.

HUSBAND *(takes her hand. We hear a roller coaster).* Just hold on to me.

END

GUNSLINGER MOTEL
by
Erik Ramsey

CHARACTERS

DICK: Works the night desk at the Gunslinger Motel, 58.

RUSTY: An out-of-work cowhand, 56.

PLACE: A small Western town.

TIME: The present.

GUNSLINGER MOTEL

SETTING: *A small, dingy motel lobby containing a desk with an old manual typewriter, a ratty love seat, a coffee table covered with decrepit magazines, and walls decorated with Old West antique pieces (rifles, tomahawks, etc.).*

AT RISE: *DICK is typing at the desk. He stops, removes the paper and reads silently to himself, obviously pleased. When he stands up from his desk chair we can see he has a severe limp due to a genetic deformity in his left leg. DICK strides unevenly to the back wall where he removes a giant black cowboy hat and a gunbelt with a Colt revolver from their display hooks. After adorning himself, he turns to face the audience and addresses them as if addressing his own reflection in a large picture window. He uses an animated voice, almost like a sportscaster.*

DICK. The deadly still, deserted main street was empty and calm, the air hanging motionless. Dust devils chased the rolling tumbleweeds. The thirteen notches in the pearl handles of his twin Colts, five in the left and six in the right, itched for another kill. Mick Gordon sauntered brazenly into the street and faced Red Trusty as they had been destined to do. In a flash, he drew! *(DICK draws his revolver.)* There was a loud report!

The dust and smoke refused to settle for too long a moment. *(DICK reholsters the gun.)* All too soon it became apparent that Red Trusty had vanquished the scurvy dog with the pureness of his heart as transmuted through the mastery of his gun-metal. *(DICK takes off the cowboy hat and scratches his head, talking to himself in his normal voice.)* No, no, no. Too flowery there at the end.

(He places the hat back on his head and prepares to draw again. RUSTY limps in behind him, unnoticed, and watches as DICK draws.)

DICK. There was a loud report! The dust and smoke refused to settle for too long a moment. Suddenly it became apparent that Red Trusty had vanquished the loathsome Mick Gordon with a pure heart pumping deadly gouts of lead. *(RUSTY bursts into laughter and applause. He is in his socks, his left ankle is wrapped in bandages, his hair is matted and his clothes look slept in.)*

RUSTY. Brave-oh, brave-oh!

DICK *(removes his hat and gunbelt, returning to his desk)*. Oh, hello, Rusty. I, uh, didn't hear you come in.

RUSTY. I noticed.

DICK. Don't mind me. What can I do for you?

RUSTY. I kinda wondered exactly what you did in here at four in the morning.

DICK. Is that why you came in?

RUSTY. What?... Oh, shit, no. You know the guy staying in 36?

DICK. He seems nice enough. Been here ten days on that workover up on Hamilton Dome.//
RUSTY. He ain't queer, is he?//
DICK. Sorry?//
RUSTY. You don't think he might be a homosexual, do you? I mean, not that they ain't got their rights and such, but he ain't, is he?//
DICK. I don't know. Is he bothering you?//
RUSTY. Well, actually, he might be the one to come complaining about *me* tomorrow.//
DICK. Yeah?//
RUSTY. Well, I don't never lock the door to my room you know.//
DICK. What does this have to do with the guy in 36?//
RUSTY. He might be a little sore at me.//
DICK. Why?//
RUSTY. Well, I, well, you seen me come in about 2:30?//
DICK. Yeah, about then.//
RUSTY. How'd I look?//
DICK. Almost as bad as you do now.//
RUSTY. That's almost unkind.//
DICK. You asked.//
RUSTY. That fella in 36 must be a pretty deep sleeper.//
DICK. Christ, Rusty! Speak your piece!//
RUSTY. Well, I was about three-quarter blind and the other half was all fogged up. I found the door knob and it wasn't locked so I just slipped in, tossed off my hat and fell on the sheets.//
DICK. And?//
RUSTY. Well, my room is 38, ain't it?

DICK. Did you climb into bed with the guy in 36?
RUSTY. I believe I did.
DICK. He didn't wake up?
RUSTY. Nope. Not right off. He just now got up and went to the toilet a little while ago. The flush woke me. I kinda froze up wondering what in the name of Jerusalem was going on. Then he comes back to the bed and kisses me real gentle on the forehead and says he loves me and he goes back to sleep. He was real tender about the whole thing. But I surmise he thought I was his wife 'cause the alternative would make me itchy the rest of my days.
DICK. Dammit, Rusty! He didn't hear you leave?
RUSTY. No.
DICK. If you're lucky, maybe he won't remember. You know what happened the last time Judge Byner sentenced you for public intoxication.
RUSTY. I know. That's why I come to you.
DICK. There's nothing I can do about it. I can't help you with the fact that you try to drink and fight like a twenty year old. Do you realize how ridiculous you look? A man your age should be bouncing grandchildren on his knee, not bouncing out of a saloon on his face.
RUSTY. Well, see, it ain't quite that simple.
DICK. What else?
RUSTY. My crutches are still in there.
DICK. Well, go get them out and let the chips fall!
RUSTY. I would, but, well, I did him a favor on the way out of the room. I locked his door for him. I thought it

was the least I could do. Then I remembered my crutches.

DICK. I'm not going in there!

RUSTY. C'mon, Dick!

DICK. No.

RUSTY. Tricky-dicky, c'mon, Dick!

DICK. No! Look at yourself. You can't even ride a horse! That ankle should've healed up a month ago.

RUSTY. Then give me the key.

DICK. I will not.

RUSTY. Be a pal, Dick.

DICK. Absolutely not.

RUSTY *(turns and faces DICK abruptly).* I could just take it from you, you gimp.

DICK. Look who's talking. Get out of my office.

RUSTY *(pause).* Dang. I'm sorry, Dick. That wasn't fair of me.

DICK. Out.

RUSTY. My niece says I'm an asshole because I was raised without women in my life.

DICK. That's convenient.

RUSTY. You're right. I apologize.

DICK. Whatever. I got some work I have to— *(RUSTY cuts him off.)*

RUSTY. How old you think I am?

DICK. What?

RUSTY. How old you think I am?

DICK. I... I don't... I don't know, forty-nine?

RUSTY. Fifty-goddamn-six.

DICK. I'll be fifty-eight in February.

RUSTY. Shit. We've done just about pissed out all the vinegar, ain't we?

DICK. I guess so.

RUSTY. You wouldn't know it to look at me now but I was a hell of a sight once.

DICK. Don't sell yourself short. You're still a hell of a sight.

RUSTY. No, I mean way back when. Heck, I didn't even have to look good, Bandit was enough of a pussy magnet himself. Beautiful goddamn horse.

DICK *(looking at his watch).* Jeez, I better get back to—

RUSTY. Shoshoni pony. He had a crescent-shaped blaze on his chest like he was wearing a bandanna around his neck. That's why I called him Bandit.

DICK. I really ought to get things—

RUSTY. I shot him in the head.

DICK. Say again?

RUSTY. I shot him in the head.

DICK. The guy in 36?

RUSTY. No, Bandit. Jesus, Dick!

DICK. Well, how the hell am I supposed to—

RUSTY. You and your goddamn words!

DICK. What?

RUSTY. You think you can just play with my brain because you been gimped up all your life and it forced ya to stay indoors and read books!

DICK. Maybe you should go back and get some sleep.

RUSTY. You *write* books too, don't you?

DICK. Well, yes, but that's—

RUSTY. I heard what you were saying before. That was from your book.

DICK. So?

RUSTY. Let me read it.

DICK. Not on your life.

RUSTY. You don't actually like me much, do you?

DICK. Not much, no.

RUSTY. But I'm your goddamn hero.

DICK *(pause)*. What were you saying about Bandit?

RUSTY. Say that part again. That part you were saying when I walked in here.

DICK. Why did you shoot Bandit?

RUSTY. Put on the hat and the pistola and say it again.

DICK. If you'll tell me why you shot Bandit.

RUSTY. You can't even stop now, can you?

DICK. Stop what?

RUSTY. Taking notes. When you first come out here I thought you were a complete idiot. Leaving some decent job in Denver to come work the night shift at the Gunslinger Motel does not seem like smarts to me. But I watched you watching me. And then I stole a couple of pages of your typing when you were in the crapper one night.

DICK. I wondered where those went.

RUSTY. Look...I shot Bandit because I had to. It was my responsibility. He was an old fucker. My buddy Tommy told me not to take the animal packing up into the Bighorns, but I was thickheaded about the whole thing. *(Pause.)* Busted his leg in a boulder field comin' off the pass from Lost Twin Lakes. I guess me and that six-point across his back was too much for his old bones. Tommy offered to do the deed. 'Course I up and hit him in the mouth. If anybody's gonna put an animal of mine out of its misery, it's gonna be me.

DICK. What are you saying?

RUSTY. Just a story. Did you get it all memorized for your book?

DICK. Are you saying something about my handicap?

RUSTY. Shit, Dick. Your hero's name is Red Trusty. I read it the other night. He's the one who saves damsels in distress. I thought it seemed kinda hokey because there ain't really no good guys going around being heroes. Never was. But the name struck me funny. It rhymes exactly with the name my own mother gave to me. Then I read on a little further and find the villain's name is Mick Gordon. Ain't your last name Jordan? Dick Jordan?

DICK. I've got things I have to do, Rusty.

RUSTY. Now, I got the biggest kick of all out of that. Who would ever write a book and put himself as the bad guy? And just a minute ago I heard you tell it that Red Trusty shoots Mick Gordon. I can see why you'd put me in as the hero since I'm probably the only real cowboy you ever met. But make yourself out to be the villain? And then I shoot you?

DICK. What do you know about writing anyway?

RUSTY. Very little and that's a fact. But I do know about cowboys.

DICK. What's your point, Rusty? Do you have a point, or are you going to just stand there and teach me how to write?

RUSTY. There was a time when I would have busted you in the mouth, handicap or not, just for the tone in your voice. But I'm well beyond that now... Yeah, I told you that story about Bandit for a reason.

DICK. And?

RUSTY. Being a useless disfigured son of a bitch doesn't hurt *your* job, Dick. Doesn't get in *your* way. Sure, you're an ugly fucker, but being a gimp is no harm to a guy with enough smarts who makes his living from his head.

DICK. I'm flattered.

RUSTY. But there's things you can never know about fully because you never did 'em. You don't know shit about roping or riding fences, except what I tell you. Well, I'm going to help you finish that book of yours the right way, right now. You want to tell stories about cowboys, you better *feel* what it's like to be one... I'm not much of a step up from Bandit when he was lying there in that boulder field, and I know it. So I figure we can help each other out.

DICK. I'm not sure... I... What do you want from me?

RUSTY. *I* need you to be a cowboy for a minute. A real one. And *you* need to be a cowboy for your book.

DICK. What are you asking me to do?

RUSTY. Put on that gunbelt and that hat again.

DICK. Why?

RUSTY. Strap on the pistola and we'll work through how the story should end.

DICK. I don't know, Rusty—

RUSTY. Do it! Now!

DICK. Jesus Christ, all right! *(DICK straps on the gun and plops the hat on his head.)*
RUSTY. Square off on me now, like you have them doing in the story. *(DICK and RUSTY move opposite each other and begin to flex their hands at their sides.)* Good. That's right. Now, when I say draw, you draw.
DICK. I feel kind of silly.
RUSTY. You don't look any sillier than you did when I walked in here.
DICK. Yeah, but I thought I was alone.
RUSTY. Draw! *(RUSTY raises his right arm quickly, pointing at DICK. DICK stays motionless.)* Draw, I said!... You goddam worthless piece-of-no-good-coyote-loving-turd! Draw and finish the story the way it ought to be finished!... I was a real cowboy, you greasy saddle sore, and I never worked with nor met another cowboy who had the nickname "Kid"! The meanest, toughest hombre and the finest ranch hand I ever saw rode a Yamaha—not an appaloosa. He wore a baseball cap, not a ten-gallon felt bucket! You cock-eyed, half-assed bent-leg big-head gimp! *(Pause.)*
DICK. You're a pretty tough critic, Rusty. Maybe you ought to take a writing workshop. *(DICK draws.)* There was a loud report. It echoed again and again across the flat sagebrush plains until it reached the ears of nature's undertakers, the buzzards, where they napped in the downy boudoir of the heavens. The brisk breeze cleared the smoke smoldering from his gun barrels. The nefarious Gordon lingered laughing as he gloated above the pitiful pile which once was Red Trusty... *(DICK lowers*

the gun.) I owe you an apology, Rusty. That might be one of the most lyrical paragraphs that ever came out of me.

RUSTY. Good. I'm glad.

DICK. No, really! That was fantastic! I gotta get that on paper.

RUSTY. You ain't done yet.

DICK. What?

RUSTY. Finish it.

DICK. I did. That's one of the finest pieces of writing I've ever done.

RUSTY. No. Pull the trigger.

DICK. You're not serious.

RUSTY. Point that thing at my chest and pull the trigger. You owe me that. *(DICK's hand shakes as he draws a bead on RUSTY. He pulls the trigger and there's only a loud click.)*

DICK. I'm... I... I'm sorry, Rusty. The barrel is soldered shut. This here's just a museum piece. *(DICK lowers the gun. RUSTY stares at the floor for a beat, then turns and begins to limp back to his room, and at the same time he pulls a comb from his back pocket and combs his hair as he exits. Lights fade.)*

END

BUZZ
by
Mark Steven Jensen

CHARACTERS

JUDY: A married woman in her 60s.

PETE: Judy's husband, also in his 60s.

PLACE: Judy and Pete's bedroom.

TIME: Present day, late in the evening.

BUZZ

AT RISE: *PETE and JUDY in their bedroom. They wear what they normally wear to bed. Sound of a fly.*

JUDY. Swat the lousy thing! I wanna get to bed.
PETE. Sh! The fly has to land. When it lands I'll swat it. It can't stay in the air forever. *(The fly buzzes.)*
JUDY. Don't move around so much!
PETE. I have to be close by when it stops.
JUDY. It won't land with you shaking the air.
PETE. The only way it'll land is if you are quiet.
JUDY. Flies can't hear.
PETE. Yes, they can.
JUDY. They don't have ears.
PETE. The vibrations. They sense sound vibrations.
JUDY. What do you know about flies?
PETE. I read all about them in *National Geographic*.
JUDY. You read your *National Geographic*? I thought you just looked at the pictures. Pictures of topless tribal women.
PETE. As if you know what I read. You don't know what I'm doing or thinking most times.
JUDY. We've never talked to each other this way. It's terrible.
PETE. Forget it, forget it. We're just cranky and tired.
JUDY. I saw you eyeing that girl today at 7-Eleven. Y'know, she didn't even look back at you. *(PETE swats at the fly. He trips and stubs his toe.)* Women

don't look at you anymore. So you shouldn't keep on like that. You're a foolish old fart if you think you can still do things like that. You stub your toe?

PETE. Boy, I'll say.

JUDY. I could get some ice.

PETE. No, no. Throbbing's already easing up.

JUDY. I'll get you some. It'll get swollen.

PETE. You say our fly swatter is in the garage?

JUDY. It's under a pile of junk somewhere.

PETE. I'll look for it.

JUDY. You're going to clean the garage over a fly?

PETE. I'll just scab around and see if I can find it.

JUDY. Let's open the window. I can shoosh it outside.

PETE. Do that, then. I'll be in the garage.

JUDY. Not in your pajamas. Or what you call your pajamas. Next thing will be you, a doctor, and pneumonia. *(She opens the window.)*

PETE. Be just as cold in here with that window wide open. *(JUDY starts chasing the fly.)*

JUDY. Might even be colder. *(Silence while PETE watches JUDY's efforts.)*

PETE. So you watched me look over that girl at 7-Eleven?

JUDY. Whoosh! Out the window.

PETE. You aren't making any progress, settle down now. Judy, you stop that now. *(JUDY stops.)* You could at least respect that I got some vim. I like young women, yes, it's their energy I like most. They remind me of... Forget it, just forget all about it. Hey, shh! Look at that, I can squash the thing. It's landed on the dresser. *(PETE grabs JUDY's romance novel.)*

JUDY. You can't use my book! That's my favorite book.
PETE. The last one was your favorite book.
JUDY. It's my favorite book right now.
PETE. I'll scrape off what gets on it. *(PETE holds the book over the night table. JUDY grabs his arm and the book.)* Judy!
JUDY. You can't use it! *(Fly buzzes.)*
PETE. Now it's... Those books are chuck full of smut. At least I don't read about suave Juan and his penetrating...passion!
JUDY. My books ain't like that.
PETE. I read that in one of them.
JUDY. You did not.
PETE. Where did I read that then?
JUDY. *National Geographic.* Let's go back to bed. It'll fly out after a little while, if—if—we just ignore it. We've got it all riled up and it doesn't know which way to go. It just wants to get outside.
PETE. We could try that, I suppose.
JUDY. Get the light, please.
PETE. Yeah, yeah. *(Switches off light.)* Good night, Judy.
JUDY. Uh-uh. *(Tense kiss. They settle down. The fly buzzes. The fly buzzes some more. The fly buzzes still more. PETE sits up.)* Patience, Pete. You never have enough patience.
PETE. Buzz. Buzz. Buzz.
JUDY. Shh, Peter! *(The fly lands on the lamp beside PETE. He slowly moves his hand towards the lamp, watching JUDY carefully as well. Finally he feels close enough*

to the fly and whacks the lamp. The lamp falls on the floor. The fly buzzes. JUDY is not pleased.)

PETE. I barely tapped it!

JUDY. You've never liked that lamp. You've always hated it. It's busted, ain't it? That lamp was an anniversary present from my uncle Seymour.

PETE. It was a Christmas present.

JUDY. He gave it to us for our anniversary.

PETE. He gave it to you for Christmas. Our first Christmas.

JUDY. It was an anniversary present.

PETE. No, it wasn't.

JUDY. It was. I remember sitting with Mother while you were out drinking with the boys. I opened the package and he was there and I said what a wonderful lamp this is.

PETE. I know it was Christmas but it's one of those things we just won't get an answer to because your uncle Seymour's been dead fourteen years!

JUDY. It's a beautiful lamp. I don't see what's wrong with it.

PETE. Well, the thing's not broke.

JUDY. You hit my lamp that hard so you could break it and get rid of it. That's your way.

PETE *(turns on the lamp)*. See, the anniversary present you got at Christmas is not broke. Still. *(They both sit on the bed. The fly buzzes. They don't react.)* I did mean what I said today, even though I said I didn't.

JUDY. I could tell.

PETE. I knew you could tell. I've known that all night.

JUDY. You thinking about leaving?

PETE. Just thinking.

JUDY. Am I that bad?

PETE. When you want to be. Then, so am I, too.

JUDY. Tonight doesn't count. You got me in this mood.

PETE. Yes, yes, and I am exaggerating, always exaggerating...

JUDY. What do we do with the house?

PETE. I don't know.

JUDY. Our kids. The little grandkids.

PETE. Don't you ever want out? *(Fly buzzes.)* For a year maybe. Another city. You by yourself. Me by myself. What would that be like, anyway?

JUDY. Thirty years, Peter. We've been...thirty years. *(Fly noise.)* That fly is gonna keep us up all night.

PETE. I just have to grab that last bit of fire, taste the sun on some beach maybe. I've got ten, maybe fifteen good years left. I could still...still...

JUDY. That fly is too much! *(JUDY, upset, frantically swats the walls.)*

PETE. Judy. Judy!

JUDY. You think I like being this way? Older? I just can't help it, Pete, I just can't. Are you really going to be able to find anyone better?

PETE. Doubt there'll be somebody else. That's foolish thinking. *(Fly buzzes.)*

JUDY. Let's get rid of that filthy fly before we talk about this anymore. Okay?

PETE. Sure. If you want.

JUDY. Maybe we can pen it in a corner. Here, use your magazine, I'll use my book. *(Both armed, they prowl around the room.)* It's over this way. *(They sneak carefully towards it. PETE stands poised with his magazine. JUDY nods for him to go. PETE slams the book down hard. Fly buzzes. JUDY flails her book in the air. The fly gets away.)* We're hopeless.

PETE. We came at it from the wrong angle. Flies jump backwards before they get in the air. We came at it towards its head. Slippery thing. *(Fly buzzes.)* I don't hate you, Judy. You do know that.

JUDY. No, I didn't know that.

PETE. There's only been irritation and more irritation between us lately. I... I can't stand that. *(They are quiet.)*

JUDY. Remember when we began? Our dates at the fair. They've gotten me through all our troubles, even these. Now those were times. The ice cream cones. The Ferris wheel and the merry-go-round. Early days. When will you leave?

PETE. I hadn't...hadn't thought it through that far. Really. I don't even know where I would go.

JUDY. Maybe a trip by yourself. You just go somewhere alone. Would that help?

PETE. Somewhere alone?

JUDY. Yes.

PETE. Without you?

JUDY. That would probably feel just like heaven.

PETE. Don't talk that way. I'm just missing something. Whatever that is, it has to come back. Maybe...it can come back with you. And maybe it can't. *(Fly buzzes.)*

JUDY. Pete, I gotta know what it will be like. Will I have you tomorrow, or will you be planning to go? I need to know right now, you see. If there'll be a change coming from you, I gotta be ready for what'll...happen.

PETE. The fair was a glorious time.

JUDY. Yes it was. *(PETE tries to swat the fly. He misses and chases it. Stern:)* Leave the fly be. Pete. You owe me a choice. Make one. *(Long silence.)*

PETE. Let's bring back the fair.

JUDY. I don't know if we can.

PETE. We have to.

JUDY. Yes. We do. *(Fly buzzes.)*

PETE. Better keep the window open. The fly might get outside then.

JUDY. It'll be too cold in here.

PETE. There's always the living room. With the big sofa. And the fireplace.

JUDY. You'll start the fireplace?

PETE. I'll start the fireplace.

JUDY. Okay. Well.

PETE. Well.

JUDY. Then start stacking the wood. I'll get the matches.

PETE. We won't sleep much tonight.

JUDY. No.

PETE. I better bring in a lot of wood.

JUDY. Thanks for the chance.

PETE. It's much more than a chance. *(They squeeze hands briefly and leave. The fly buzzes.)*

END

PAPER WALLS
by
Jenny Laird

CHARACTERS

ISABELLA "IZZY" MANCHEE: In her 60s, sort of petite and spunky. She dresses in "frocks" and although she never has visitors she still puts on lipstick every morning.

BERTRAM MANCHEE: In his 60s. He looks a bit dishevelled, or perhaps more like a man who has never heard of an iron.

PLACE: Izzy and Bert's apartment.

TIME: The present. Summer.

PAPER WALLS

SETTING: *Izzy and Bert's second-floor apartment is filled with major amounts of "stuff," and above all else, looks lived in. The brown corduroy couch is fluffy and old and covered with various doilies and throw blankets. The old television set has rabbit ears and knobs (remember those?). They've no use for a remote control because they turn it on one channel in the morning and it stays that way until bedtime. The clothes IZZY packs are anything but stylish, and the suitcase she uses looks like it was salvaged from World War II.*

AT RISE: *IZZY is packing a suitcase. BERT is fiddling with the back of the television set.*

BERT. Izzy, come on. I can get her fixed.
IZZY. That's what you said last night.
BERT. It's a fuse, I'm sure of it. Now, I just gotta figure out which one, is all.
IZZY. Well I'm not missin' *Final Jeopardy* tonight.
BERT. "You ain't heard nothin' yet."
IZZY. Huh?
BERT. That was the answer, or the question, or whatever it is on that show.
IZZY. How do you know? It went all fuzzy before Alec even asked the question, or gave the answer...oh, now you got me all confused.

BERT. It was a repeat. "Al Jolson says this in the *Jazz Singer*." And, Izzy, for the last time it's ALEX, not ALEC. ALEX SAJACK.

IZZY. So, was the *Jazz Singer* the answer or the question?

BERT. For Pete's sake, I don't know! All I remember is the lady from Louisiana gets it right.

IZZY. Oh, the lady from Louisiana. You liked her, did you?

BERT. I've always been a sucker for a southern accent.

IZZY. Stop fussin' with that thing and get packin'. I made reservations at the Motel 6.

BERT. You don't make reservations at the Motel 6.

IZZY. How would you know?

BERT. I don't know. You just know some things, Izz, like YOU know to shave your legs when you go to the doctor.

IZZY. Well, I made reservations.

BERT. Cancel them.

IZZY. They're EXPECTING us.

BERT. This is a perfectly good TV, Izzy.

IZZY. That nice little man's leaving the light on for us.

BERT. I'll get her workin', have faith in me, Bella.

IZZY. You're gonna electrocute yourself is what you're gonna do. *(IZZY exits to retrieve her toiletries, and we hear sensuous moaning.)*

BERT. What'd you say, Morty?

(IZZY enters carrying her things to pack.)

IZZY. I didn't say anything. *(We hear the sounds again.)*

BERT *(smiling)*. Must be new neighbors.

IZZY. We should've bought a new TV when Sears had 'em on sale. *(The moan grows more intense throughout.)*

BERT. I'm gonna get my tools. *(BERT purposefully searches through a cabinet against the wall where the sounds are coming from.)*

IZZY. Maybe someone oughta call the fire station.

BERT. Didn't I always want to be a fireman?

IZZY. Well it's a good thing I made reservations, no one in the neighborhood's gonna get to sleep tonight.

BERT. I woulda nicknamed myself "Smoky."

IZZY. You don't nickname yourself, Bert. Other people give you your nicknames.

BERT. Smoky Bert Manchee. *(Pause.)* What was it you used to call me, Bella? *(We hear crashing sounds and then laughter.)*

IZZY. With that kind of ruckus, I have a mind to call the police.

BERT. Izzy, you don't put your neighbors on *America's Most Wanted* for...for, you know....

IZZY. No, I don't know, Bert. I haven't the foggiest idea what two people do to make THOSE kinds of noises.

BERT. Then why're your cheeks all red?

IZZY. Do you want me to pack your blue slacks?

BERT. All I hear is the music.

IZZY. Fine job they're doing tryin' to cover it up.

BERT. Guess it's just your natural glow. *(Returning to the TV.)* I'm thinkin' now it's the wiring.

IZZY. We've got to get checked in before...before... what's that program? Comes on right after *Cops*.
BERT. I don't know, I get them all confused.
IZZY. The one where they gave mouth to snout resuscitation to that deer. *(BERT, as if answering a* Jeopardy *question.)*
BERT. *Rescue 911?*
IZZY. Yeah. *Rescue 911.* Well tonight they're gonna show that huge man who has a heart attack.
BERT. Another repeat.
IZZY. Remember? He was so fat the little ambulance people had to saw around his door to fit him out on the stretcher.
BERT. Izzy, please stop packin'. I've almost got this figured out.
IZZY. What'd she say?
BERT. Huh?
IZZY. I don't know, I thought I heard her say something.
BERT. What, like a real word?
IZZY. A whole string of 'em, and she didn't sound happy.
BERT. Uh oh.
IZZY. Whaddya think happened?
BERT. I don't know. Maybe he...maybe he called her... Jane.
IZZY. So.
BERT. Maybe her name's Maybelle.
IZZY. Hold on...shhh. Listen.
BERT. Izzy, that's rude.
IZZY. You're the one sittin' there with your ears pricked like a wild animal.

BERT. I've got big ears, that's all. There's a difference between having big ears and eavesdropping.

IZZY *(with a glass to the wall)*. I'm not eavesdropping. I'm being subjected to the noise pollution so rampant in this city.

BERT. You used to like my ears.

IZZY. When a car honks its horn and I hear it, is it my fault?

BERT. I never realized how noisy this neighborhood is.

IZZY. That's because you got that thing turned up so loud.

BERT. You're the one who turns it on in the morning.

IZZY. I adjust the volume for you, not me. YOU.

BERT. I'm the one with big ears. I hear fine.

IZZY. A person can hardly think with the volume on that thing.

BERT. Oh, so now I don't let you think?

IZZY. Did I say that?

BERT. In so many words, you said that. You think I can't do nothin' no more. Why don't you just say it.

IZZY. All right. I think you can't do nothin' no more. Happy now?

BERT. Is that what you told the man at the Motel 6? "Yes, hello, sir, my husband can't get our TV working, you think we could move in where other people take care of that sort of thing?"

IZZY. How'd you know? You musta been eavesdropping on my conversation!

BERT. I was not eavesdropping! *(BERT slams his fist on top of the TV and the picture turns completely clear.)* Ah hah. See there. I'm good for something.

IZZY. You're a grumpy old man is what you are!
BERT. Grumpy! How can I help being grumpy living with a stubborn old woman!
IZZY. Stubborn! I'll show you stubborn! *(IZZY slams her suitcase shut and goes to the door, opening it to exit.)* YOU can watch TV alone tonight! *(Just as IZZY is about to exit, the sound of a door slamming can be heard.)*
BERT *(in unison)*. Uh oh.
IZZY *(in unison)*. Uh oh.
BERT. Listen. *(IZZY quietly closes the door.)*
IZZY *(whispering)*. What?
BERT. The music stopped. *(They listen to the silence.)* Sure is quiet.
IZZY. With these whippersnappers, you never know. Tempers flare, passions rise, you never know what's comin' next.
BERT. One minute it's one thing, the next it's another.
IZZY. She'll be back any minute.
BERT. She...she probably forgot her purse, and she'll come back to get it and—
IZZY. And he'll apologize—
BERT. Say it's all his fault—
IZZY. Which it is—
BERT. Even though it's probably just her nerves—
IZZY. Which he has a habit of gettin' on—
BERT. Or maybe it was him that left.
IZZY. You never know...
BERT. They don't know yet, life is a compromise.
IZZY. You win some, you lose some.

BERT. But you never slam doors.

IZZY. And you never go to bed angry.

BERT. Worked for us. *(There is an awkward silence.)*

IZZY. I wonder what Vanna's wearing tonight? *(BERT turns off the TV. He grabs a stack of old albums and searches through.)* What're you pullin' out those old dust balls for?

BERT. Let's see if we can get those two together again.

IZZY. Bertram, I don't even think that thing works anymore.

BERT. Oh it works all right, we just need to plug it in. *(He unplugs the TV and plugs in an old record player.)*

IZZY *(laughing)*. Remember that first apartment we lived in?

BERT. The one with paper walls.

IZZY. Yeah. And they called the super on us for playing Sinatra over and over.

BERT. Who was it? Old lady Ida made us pay her doctor bill.

IZZY. Told the shrink she thought she was living the same hour over and over.

BERT. I could hear her singing "My Way" in the shower.

IZZY. She had a decent voice.

BERT. In the shower. Come here, Isabella Manchee.

IZZY. Wait. I think he's back.

BERT. Probably just went for Chinese.

IZZY. She had a craving for moo goo gai pan.

BERT. And pickles.

IZZY. I always craved salt... back then.

BERT. My little Morton salt girl.

IZZY *(with her ear to the wall)*. Hurry. Find a song before he leaves again! *(BERT turns on Louie Armstrong's "A Kiss to Build a Dream On.")*

BERT. Ahhh...remember... *(They sing the words to the wall as if wishing the neighbors would hear and understand.)*

IZZY. "Give me a kiss to build a dream on..."

BERT. "and my imagination will thrive upon that kiss—"

IZZY. "Sweetheart, I ask no more than this..."

BERT. "a kiss to build a dream on." *(Both are swaying, lost in the reverie. They hear the sounds of lovemaking again.)* Dance with me, Morty.

IZZY. Morty?

BERT. The girl with the umbrella and salty skin. *(IZZY smiles and holds out her hand, They begin dancing.)*

IZZY *(in a southern accent, fanning herself)*. Mr. Smoky Bert Manchee, I do believe there's a fire needs putting out. *(BERT kisses IZZY. As the lights fade, SMOKY BERT and MORTY dance as if they were twenty.)*

END

SOME SAY FIRE
by
Erik Ramsey

CHARACTERS

MRS. BINDLE: Owns a motel with a bar attached, 66.

HARVEY: A handyman, 71.

PLACE: A small Western town.

TIME: The present.

SOME SAY FIRE

SETTING: *A large ice machine, its various wires and electrical innards strewn about wildly across its face and onto the floor.*

AT RISE: *HARVEY is fiddling with the wires from the ice machine. MRS. BINDLE is watching him from a bar stool, sipping a mimosa. A toolbox is at her feet.*

HARVEY. I don't think we got juice to the filaments.
MRS. BINDLE. Do you know about ignition?
HARVEY. See, it won't cut up into cubes without juice to the filaments.
MRS. BINDLE. I see.
HARVEY. You hand me the needlenose?
MRS. BINDLE. Which?
HARVEY. The needlenose.
MRS. BINDLE. Uhh... *(She leans over her drink, but HARVEY retrieves the pliers himself.)* You seem to know your trade, Harvey.
HARVEY. Yes ma'am.
MRS. BINDLE. Lyle was useless except for the taps.
HARVEY. Uh-huh.
MRS. BINDLE. He had a notion for those old taps. You probably wonder about it.
HARVEY. About what, ma'am?

MRS. BINDLE. Oh, hell, Lyle, I guess. And what business I have with this business at my age. And where my husband is.

HARVEY. No ma'am. I mind my own.

MRS. BINDLE. Lyle was our postman. Be good to a civil servant and he'll remember you, my Don always said. Well, I'd pull a draft every day about 2:30. He'd drop the mail on the bar and then gulp it and go. Then one day he asks for a second glass, this was about eight years back, right after Don died. I didn't know if I should charge him for a second glass. And before I knew it he was sloppy, and on the pay phone retiring from the force.

HARVEY. He was a policeman?

MRS. BINDLE. No, a postman. Mailman.

HARVEY. Oh.

MRS. BINDLE. I could see you'd be curious. Well, that's both good and bad, Harvey. But you're polite so I'm forced to trust you. Don't forget our arrangement though.

HARVEY. I think you just have a short in the leader to the filaments.

MRS. BINDLE. I'm happy about that, Harvey, but I can't get ahead of myself here.

HARVEY. We'll know in a second.

MRS. BINDLE. Lyle was fine for the taps but he couldn't do as I asked. He couldn't fully service my needs around this place. I have a good feeling about you, though.

HARVEY. I'll just tape these wires back together and we'll know.

MRS. BINDLE. It goes back to my Don's ideas about business. You know about diversification?

HARVEY. Ma'am?

MRS. BINDLE. Well, we wanted to buy a motel anyway, but Don says it shouldn't be just a motel it should have a bar attached. Except Don didn't call them bars he called them saloons. He wanted a cafe attached too. Thank God he never found one with a cafe attached. I just know I'd have been serving eggs on top of all the beer I pour. I can't stand the look or smell of yolk.

HARVEY. Yes ma'am.

MRS. BINDLE. You are so polite, Harvey! Where did you say you're from?

HARVEY. I don't believe I said, ma'am.

MRS. BINDLE. Oh... Oh... I see. Well... I see then.

HARVEY *(pause)*. Omaha originally. Born in Omaha.

MRS. BINDLE. Ugly city. But all those insurance companies. You ever work in insurance, Harvey?

HARVEY. No ma'am.

MRS. BINDLE. Too bad. I could use a hand figuring my fire and hazard deductible.

HARVEY. I suppose I could look at it, if you like.

MRS. BINDLE. Honestly, Harvey, your manners! They give me chills up my spine. How are we coming?

HARVEY. Any minute now. Unless I find more bad wires. It almost looks like they've been tampered with.

MRS. BINDLE. How old are you, Harvey?

HARVEY. Does it make a difference as to whether I get the job?

MRS. BINDLE. I don't know until you tell me.

Some Say Fire

HARVEY. I'm fifty-eight.

MRS. BINDLE. What year were you born?

HARVEY. Uhh...

MRS. BINDLE. I don't have a mandatory retirement age, Harvey.

HARVEY. I'm seventy-one.

MRS. BINDLE. Splendid.

HARVEY. S'cuse me?

MRS. BINDLE. I assume you remember the Depression pretty well then?

HARVEY. Sure, yeah.

MRS. BINDLE. I preferred the Depression to this recession. At least folks cared about one another. Gave out soup and such. Not anymore. Until the day he passed, my Don, bless his burning soul, would give a fiver to a drunk on a bet before he'd pay out the loans. I couldn't sell this place for a third of what I'm still paying on it.

HARVEY. I'm sorry, Mrs. Bindle, but I've found more shorts here in these wires. Maybe I could fetch you when I have it up and running?

MRS. BINDLE. Oh. I apologize, Harvey. I do rattle on sometimes. But because of Lyle I think it's for the best if I watch until you're finished.

HARVEY. You're the boss.

MRS. BINDLE. It all must seem mysterious to you by now.

HARVEY *(standing up to confront her)*. Mrs. Bindle, I am a good mechanic. I ain't much else.

MRS. BINDLE. I'm sure of that, Harvey. But who wouldn't be curious by now?

HARVEY. Look, lady, you said that if I could fix the ice machine you'd pay me handsome. That's all I'm thinking now. Handsome. That's all.

MRS. BINDLE. Of course you are. Of course. But Lyle couldn't do it, so I'm suspicious until it's done. I look inside and see all those veins and arteries but no heart behind... I only know that Lyle couldn't make it make ice, so he couldn't make it make fire either.

HARVEY. Fire?

MRS. BINDLE. Yes.

HARVEY. Maybe I should be going.

MRS. BINDLE. I know about you, Harvey. You better just fix the machine.

HARVEY. Ma'am?

MRS. BINDLE. That's the spirit, Harvey. I do so very much appreciate politeness.

HARVEY. What is it you know?

MRS. BINDLE. I seen you walk out of the gates yesterday.

HARVEY. That's another story from another place, Mrs. Bindle. That's no goddamn concern of yours.

MRS. BINDLE. This is a small town, Harvey. It's prudent for an innkeeper to know who's coming from behind the walls down the road.

HARVEY. This is cruelty beyond and above, Mrs. Bindle. Forty-four years, my mortgage is all up. I owe no more debts.

MRS. BINDLE. Can you make this machine make ice, Harvey?

HARVEY. That's what I been about since you called me in off the street!

MRS. BINDLE. Can you make the ice, Harvey?

HARVEY. Yes! Dammit to hell! Yes!

MRS. BINDLE. The idea came to me in a dream. I have arthritis, very bad arthritis, and I don't sleep well because of it. You ever use that Frozen Flame lotion?

HARVEY. You want me to fix the machine, or not?

MRS. BINDLE. I rub the Frozen Flame lotion on my joints before I go to bed. It's the only thing that soothes me. Ice or fire, your nerves can't tell which. This one night a month ago I was drifting off to sleep and had one of those in-between dreams where you jerk at the end because your eyes are still open.

HARVEY. I can go. I can walk out that door any time I wish.

MRS. BINDLE. This machine hasn't worked well for three or four years. In my dream I saw it making cubes—tiny, perfect, little orange cubes. Cubes of fire... But Lyle wasn't capable. He was shocked by it.

HARVEY. I'm more than a little surprised myself.

MRS. BINDLE. No. Lyle forgot to unplug the machine before he tried to fix it. He wasn't so bright but he had his secrets. Now, my Don was educated. He read poetry. He read Mr. Robert Frost to me.

HARVEY. I should be going now.

MRS. BINDLE. Mr. Robert Frost was the finest poet America has ever produced... Some say the world will end in fire, some say in ice.

HARVEY. I think there's been a mistake. I'll find my own way out. *(HARVEY turns to leave.)*

MRS. BINDLE. If you don't fix the machine, everyone will know how you robbed me and raped me.

HARVEY. Ma'am?

MRS. BINDLE. If you please, Harvey.

HARVEY. They warned us about this in reintegration class. They said people might try to use my past against me.

MRS. BINDLE. Fix the machine.

HARVEY. Prison wasn't all that bad, after twenty years or so. By then you know how everything moves there from top to bottom each moment of the day and night. That's a comfort somehow.

MRS. BINDLE. HELP! RAPE!

HARVEY. OKAY! Okay... Okay.

MRS. BINDLE. I knew you were a gentleman, Harvey. I knew it when I first laid eyes on you. If you can make it make ice, then I'm sure you can make it make fire too. I am certain of it. Do you see now, Harvey?

HARVEY. Yes ma'am.

MRS. BINDLE. And then we'll look over those insurance papers. Do you follow, Harvey?

HARVEY. If that's what you want, Mrs. Bindle.

MRS. BINDLE. I'm so pleased. So very pleased. A gentleman is so rare these days. *(A reddish fade.)*

END

"Seen"

SEEN
by
Douglas Hill

CHARACTERS

HARRIET: A woman in her 60s who has returned to college.

KEN: Her husband. In his 60s.

PLACE: The living room of Harriet and Ken's home.

TIME: The present.

SEEN

SETTING: *A living room with a front door to one side. A couch sits in the middle of the room.*

AT RISE: *KEN sits with parts of a VCR and a telephone surrounding him. HARRIET enters through the door with a soft briefcase and a handful of books. She is quickly crossing through the room when her briefcase slips from her hands and spills onto the floor.*

KEN. Oh. You're home early, aren't you? You'll never believe what happened. You know I told you I was going to put all the kids' stuff on one VCR tape? *(He notices she is collecting papers from the floor.)* Here, let me help you. The machine gave out. Can you believe it? I just get the TV fixed and the VCR tthhpt. But the good news is I think I got it working again. All it took was this one piece from the phone, and I bent it, and now it works like a charm.
HARRIET *(preoccupied)*. That's wonderful.
KEN. Yeah, but now the phone doesn't work, so I've got to go get a doohickey from the hardware store before they close. You want to go with me?
HARRIET. No, I'm exhausted.
KEN. Are you all right?
HARRIET. I'm fine.
KEN. What's wrong?

HARRIET. Nothing. I'm tired. *(Beat.)* I've just had one of those days and it wore me out. That's all.

KEN. What happened?

HARRIET. Ken.

KEN. All right—all right, You want me to get you some iced tea? Would that help?

HARRIET. I'll be fine. Please, just go to the store. *(KEN finds a piece of triplicate paper.)*

KEN. Here's one more...what's this for? *(Pause.)* You're not withdrawing...? *(Pause. She takes the paper from him.)*

HARRIET. It's not that important, Ken.

KEN. Waaaait a second here...

HARRIET. It's not a big deal. Don't blow it out of—

KEN. Since when? You're dropping out. When did this become "not a big deal"?

HARRIET. It just isn't. Go to the store so you can fix the phone.

KEN. I don't care about the phone. When did you decide you were going to do this?

HARRIET. I realized some things today while I was in class. That's all.

KEN. What? What exactly did you realize?

HARRIET. Ken, I just need some time by myself—

KEN. Did someone say something to you?

HARRIET *(spilling out of her)*. I'm not smart enough for college! All right?

KEN. Who told you that?

HARRIET. I'm smart enough to know it without someone telling me.

KEN. It's been maybe two, three weeks? You haven't even had an exam, have you?

HARRIET. No.

KEN. So, how do you know you're not smart enough? I think you ought to at least take a test—

HARRIET. Ken, you're not there. You don't... *(Beat.)*

KEN. I'm not there. And I don't...?

HARRIET. When you're an older student, they judge you. From the minute you walk in the room. They wonder why you're in a class that their friends couldn't take— because the class was full. They resent you for wasting their time with stupid questions. Questions that they already know the answers to. I can see it in their eyes. They all turn around and stare. And the teachers look at me as a threat. They don't want me in the class asking all those questions. They want their students to move along quietly and willingly like a flock of sheep being corralled toward graduation. But, Ken, I want to learn. I want to be as smart as our kids. I want to know what they're talking about. And sometimes I think it's possible. But there's got to be a chance for me to catch up. I know I haven't kept my nose in a book for the past sixty years and I'm sorry. But it doesn't mean I've wasted my life. And I don't think I'm the only one who hasn't read whoever's infernal *Paradise*. *(KEN pulls out the phone book.)* What are you doing?

KEN. What's that professor's name?

HARRIET. You're not going to call him. It won't solve anything.

KEN. He should know this. What you're telling me, he should know. This makes me—this ticks me— I'm just— He should know. I'm not going to let him treat you like this. You are smart. And if he's going to—
HARRIET. Ken—
KEN. —make you feel like you aren't, then he doesn't... You're a student. Like everyone else in that class. So if you've got a question, he needs to shut up and answer it. Give me his name.
HARRIET. Ken, you can't call—
KEN. I promise I'll do all the talking. I won't make you talk to him.
HARRIET. Ken, you can't call him. The phone doesn't work.
KEN. All right, I'm coming with you to class tomorrow. I want to meet this guy and those students—
HARRIET. No, I don't want you in the middle of this.
KEN. But you're letting them get away with—
HARRIET. Ken, they belong there. The school is set up for them—not me. I'm the fish out of water.
KEN. You aren't the only grandmother at that school.
HARRIET. I'm the only one in my classes. And I haven't seen many others on the campus. So I can't blame them for feeling like their territory has been invaded. They're not used to seeing people my age in their class, acting like students. It probably scares them. Because I know it scares me. I mean. *(Pause.)* Never mind.
KEN. Okay. Are you hungry? What did you have for lunch?
HARRIET. I had a yogurt before class. *(KEN nods.)*
KEN. I need a sandwich. Why don't you come with me?

HARRIET. I can make you something here.

KEN. No, I want to take you for a sandwich or a Coke or whatever you want. Okay? We're going to go to the student union.

HARRIET. Don't do this.

KEN. And you can give me a tour of the library afterwards.

HARRIET. Ken, I can't go back there today.

KEN. We have to.

HARRIET. I walked out of class.

KEN. I don't care. I want those kids to see us and I want them to see us on "their territory." And I want you to be seen. I'm not going to let you drop out because you feel like an outsider. You deserve to be there as much as the next person.

HARRIET. It'll be easier for everyone if I just withdraw.

KEN. What about you? Do you think quitting is going to be that easy for you? You were so excited about going back. You got me excited just by you being excited. You don't think you'll miss going to class?

HARRIET. I'll get over it.

KEN. Yeah, in a couple of weeks, you could get over it. Or maybe realize that this was just a bad day. I mean, look at it. This is nothing compared to raising three kids, moving across the country umpteen times, and putting up with me for thirty-nine years.

HARRIET. I know, but...

KEN. Then don't stop when you've just got started. The kids and I are so proud of you for this. *(Mock anger.)* Gosh darn it all to heck, we need somebody smart living in this house. And I'm so busy with the VCR and the phone and the dishwasher that I don't have time to do all the thinking. So it's time you pulled your weight around here, young missy. Unless you want to be responsible for putting everything back together—

HARRIET. Oh, all right. Shut up— I'll be the smart one.

KEN. Good. I always thought you might be.

HARRIET. I just can't go back today. All right?

KEN. On one condition. You throw away that "withdraw" thing. *(HARRIET rips the triplicate paper in half.)*

HARRIET. Now, what about the dishwasher...?

KEN. Uhh... Don't ask.

HARRIET. I want to know about the dishwasher.

KEN. The piece from the dishwasher broke when I bent it. That's why I took apart the phone.

HARRIET. Ken, couldn't you wait until I got home to fix the VCR? You could have saved the telephone and the dishwasher—

KEN. I wanted to surprise you. *(Beat.)* Surprise.

HARRIET. Do you think you can have everything back together tonight?

KEN. Probably.

HARRIET. All right. I'm going to go lay down and... think for a while.

KEN. Could you think about fixing a sandwich for me? Maybe?

HARRIET. I thought you were the fixer.

KEN. Do you really want me in the kitchen again?

HARRIET *(nodding)*. I'll take care of it. You stay in here. Please.

END

CONCERNED CITIZENS
by
Violet Gunter and Bob May

CHARACTERS

WANDA: In her early 60s.

YOLANDA: In her mid-60s.

HORTENSE: In her late 60s.

BONNIE: In her late 70s.

PLACE: A trailer park in any city.

TIME: The present, early summer, around noon.

CONCERNED CITIZENS

AT RISE: *YOLANDA is staring at her neighbor's trailer when WANDA enters.*

WANDA. Hi, Yolanda. Are you ready to go to lunch?
YOLANDA. Hi, not yet, Wanda.
WANDA. What's the matter?
YOLANDA. I've been wondering about Bonnie Rogers. I haven't seen her for several days.
WANDA. Neither have I, but I'm sure she's all right. Anybody as crabby as she is can take care of herself.
YOLANDA. That isn't a nice thing to say about anybody.
WANDA. Don't you agree?
YOLANDA. No. I realize that she seldom smiles, but she could have a lot on her mind.
WANDA. That's no excuse. When I see her and try to tell her hello, she doesn't answer, just glares at me.
YOLANDA. When you get to be her age, perhaps you'll act crabby... She doesn't have any relatives and I've never seen any friends coming to visit her.
WANDA. Stop worrying, Yolanda. *(Looks at watch.)* Look at the time. We should have been gone ten minutes ago. Don't forget, we're supposed to meet Mary and Alice... Besides, some church will take care of her.
YOLANDA. How can you be so sure? I'm going to peek into the windows of her trailer and see if I can spot her.

WANDA. It's against my better judgment, but I'll help, even if I am starving to death.
YOLANDA. Thought you were going on a diet.
WANDA. I am, commencing tomorrow.
YOLANDA. That's what you said last week.
WANDA. This time I mean it... I don't know what good it's going to do to look in Bonnie's window.
YOLANDA. If she's moving around, we'll know that she isn't ill. *(They look into windows.)* Darn, all the blinds are drawn. Hey, there's one that's torn. I can see into a room... Good heavens, it's her bedroom and she's in bed. I can't see her face.
WANDA. Let me look... Yep, it's her all right. I told you not to worry... Let's get out of here before she has us arrested for snooping.
YOLANDA. But, Wanda, why would she be in bed at this time of day? She's an early riser and it's at least 12:15.
WANDA. Beats me. If she wants to sleep her life away, that's up to her. *(She takes YOLANDA by the hand and pulls her away.)* Let's go to lunch. *(YOLANDA pulls away from WANDA and goes back to trailer.)* Yolanda, didn't you hear me?
YOLANDA. I'm going to ring the bell and wake her up.
WANDA. You're a stubborn lady. Why don't you let well enough alone.
YOLANDA. I can't. I have a funny feeling that she may need help. She may even be DEAD. *(She rings bell, then knocks on door. Both ladies start calling.)*
YOLANDA & WANDA. BONNIE—BONNIE—BONNIE—BONNIE—

(HORTENSE enters and goes up to the ladies.)

HORTENSE. What are you ladies doing? You're interrupting my favorite soap opera. I thought someone was getting murdered... You're making enough noise to wake up the dead.
WANDA. Funny you should say that, Hortense.
HORTENSE. Why?
YOLANDA. We think Bonnie Rogers is in there, DEAD.
HORTENSE. Have you ladies been drinking?
WANDA. Drinking? Do you want us to walk a straight line for you?
YOLANDA. Bonnie's in bed and isn't answering our knocks or calls. No one has seen her for several days.
HORTENSE. Maybe she just wants to sleep. *(Looks at watch.)* Damn, I'm going to miss the ending of that soap.
YOLANDA. Hortense, you and Wanda think alike. I believe we should be good neighbors and find out whether she needs any help.
WANDA. I don't think we should get involved.
HORTENSE. I think we should call the cops.
WANDA. What can they do?
HORTENSE. Break the door down and find out whether anything is wrong.
YOLANDA. Let's call the police. If I were sick and lived alone, I'd appreciate it if someone was interested and worried enough to help me.
WANDA. How can anyone help her if she's dead?... Of course, we could take up a collection for flowers.

BONNIE'S VOICE *(offstage)*. Thanks for the ride.
HORTENSE. Speaking of the devil.
WANDA. It's the old crab herself. She doesn't look dead.

(BONNIE comes in, limping up to the ladies.)

BONNIE. What the hell are you ladies doing around my trailer? Some Peeping Tom or other is always around.
YOLANDA. We were worried about you, Bonnie. Where have you been? ...Now, don't get upset, but there's a body in your bed.
BONNIE. A body? You peeped in my window?... Looks like it works... Well, Nosy Parkers, that body is a wax dummy which I stashed in my bed to make it look like a body. Can't have anyone thinking there's no one home... I've been out of town. Went to Niagara Falls.
WANDA. Where's your luggage?
BONNIE. That stupid airport misplaced it, but they said they will either find it or reimburse me for the contents. Maybe I'll get some new duds.
HORTENSE. You should let someone know when you're going to be gone.
BONNIE. Why? I can take care of myself.
YOLANDA. That's not the point. Everyone needs friends. Someday, you may need help. I'm available if you do.
WANDA. Me too.
HORTENSE. You can count on me.
BONNIE. That's wonderful. The next time I take off, I'll notify you, Yolanda. Didn't think anyone around here cared for me.

HORTENSE. I think you have more friends than you realize.

WANDA. We were going to call the police.

BONNIE. Too bad you didn't, dearies. Maybe I could have gotten a date with one of them. I looked but didn't find a beau at Niagara Falls... That's the place where honeymooners go... I'd better get inside and take a load off my feet. They've been killing me. Joe, my little mannequin will be glad to tell me all the latest news... Come see me tomorrow, and I'll show you the Polaroid pictures I took... You're all welcome. *(She exits.)*

WANDA. She isn't a crabby old thing after all.

YOLANDA. That's what I've been trying to tell you.

HORTENSE. Let's play cards this afternoon. If we need a fourth hand, we'll ask Bonnie to lend us her Joe—

WANDA. Now can we go to lunch?

END

STARMAN, WISH ME LUCK
by
Nicole J. Burton

CHARACTERS

STARMAN: In his late 50s, of compact build with a face faintly reminiscent of Uncle Sam. His animal persona is a goat. He wears black, cloven-toed boots and he has a white goatee that he keeps trimmed. He carries his possessions, which include many cardboard flags he has drawn, in a couple of knapsacks that are decorated with Magic Marker stars (the star being his personal motif). He wears a pair of camouflage pants, an army hat, and a sturdy jacket. A resident of the city streets, he is an East European refugee and has a slight accent.

CONTESSA: In her early 60s. Her animal persona is a fox and she has a foxtail that she grooms occasionally during conversation. She dresses in mismatched clothes but she has good carriage and carries it off. She's wearing a hat, a coat, and galoshes. She carries a canvas bag with crusts or cake for the pigeons, a flask and some sandwiches. She's lived in many states and a few countries, and she has a modest apartment in a four-story walk-up. An alcoholic, her moods shift easily from one extreme to another.

PLACE: A city park.

TIME: The present. Christmas Eve. Mid-afternoon.

STARMAN, WISH ME LUCK

SETTING: *On stage is a bench with a trash can next to it. A large Christmas tree decorated with lights rises behind the bench next to a life-size creche at R. It is a very cold day. [Note: There are no scene breaks.]*

AT RISE: *STARMAN is sitting on the bench, bundled up, drawing on a sheet of posterboard with a Magic Marker. He is making a flag. He has a bandage on his head under his hat. He is upset by an exchange with a police officer earlier in the day, and he mimics the officer in his first few lines. Then, he begins making a new flag on which he also writes his story. He talks to the audience and to himself.*

STARMAN. "Mighty cold out here, Billy..." "Don't be out here when I come through tonight, Billy—Mayor says we gotta pick everybody up!" *(He writes.)* Two thousand years ago, my ancestors came from India. *(He looks up.)* Now I can never go home. The stinking dogs stole my green card, my Medicaid card, and my birth certificate. It says on it that I was born in Poland. *(He laughs.)* Galicia, I was born in Lemburg, Galicia. *(He writes.)* Empirium Orium. Erikson Papalona. *(He looks up.)* When Franz Josef died, the double-headed eagle came to California and to Illinois. *(He gets up excitedly and kicks the trash can.)* Trash, trash, stupid trash! Why does everything go to hell? I went to see Nixon, I went to see Ford. The judge took the case and then he dismissed it! Morons! Fleabags! Whoremongers! *(The jumping around hurts his head and he sits down again.)* They took many flags—Galicia, Bongo-Congo, Midland. *(Directly to the audience.)* I'll freeze before I go back to that stinking shelter!

(Enter CONTESSA. She is carrying a bag of sandwiches. She sits down on the bench and begins feeding the birds.)

CONTESSA. Hello, pidgies. I'm glad to see you today. I have lots of news. Oh you're hungry, are you, darlings? Aren't they lovely, aren't they sweet? Oh look, here they come. They know my voice. They know I'm going to give them a little dry cake, don't you? They're so loyal. Oh, there's Pinkie. Pinkie-winkie! None of those awful seagulls today, Starman. *(She looks at him.)* You look glum. What happened to your head? Here, feed them some cake. *(He eats it.)*

STARMAN. What good is it to steal a man's papers?

CONTESSA. What happened?

STARMAN. Eh!

CONTESSA. Did you look in the garbage cans?

STARMAN *(looks with disdain)*. The place is a garbage can. I looked all over the place, all day.

CONTESSA. Did they get any money? *(No response.)* At least you get your check soon. Here, have a sandwich, it's liverwurst. *(He takes the sandwich reluctantly but eats with relish.)* It is miserable out here. Why don't you go down to the Harrington, get yourself a room? *(No response.)* I'm so excited, I don't know what to do. I got a letter from Gerrie in Florida yesterday. She wants me to come visit! You remember, she was the WAF. They used to come in the club I worked at. Well, she's in Boca Raton now. Never married, and she says she hasn't been feeling well, and she'd like to see me. Oh, I don't know what to do—it would be wonderful...rum and Cokes by the pool, the breezes and the moonlight...

STARMAN. I wouldn't waste a minute to go to Florida right now. It's warm. I'd drink vodka and lie in the sun... We could walk on the beach... *(They dream.)* I'd go to Florida with you!

CONTESSA. Stop it! You don't know what it means to have responsibilities. There are people watching me all the time, waiting to take over my place. Not just thieves—squatters. They break in and take over. I don't even like to go to the store anymore. Don't look at me like that.

STARMAN. You lock the door and leave. You come back. No one's going to take over your house unless *you* let them in.

CONTESSA. They watch me all the time. I should get back. I've been out since two and somebody took one of my keys last night. Can't say who but I have plenty of suspicions... *(Digging into her bag.)* Look, I got mincemeat!... I can't go. Anyway, she wants to see me, not some old goat. *(She starts to leave.)*

STARMAN. Contessa, wait, come back, please. Please *(He motions for her to sit back down.)* Stay for just a minute.

CONTESSA *(demurs, flicking her tail out from underneath her as she sits down).* Well, just for a minute. I've got to get started on my mince pie. *(Sighs.)* You know, the Count would know what to do, and he would do it with flair. *(She gets up and illustrates.)* The Count was a man of means. He knew how to light a cigarette. To open a car door. To make love to a woman. *(CONTESSA offers a cigarette to STARMAN, who accepts it, and gives him her lighter to light her cigarette. Inhaling, she continues.)* Unfortunately, he was proud. The only job he could find was in a toilet factory and he couldn't take it. In the end, the mutts of the world endure. I shouldn't say that to you, should I, Prince Starman? *(Indicating the flag he's drawing.)* That's a good one. Hang it up *(He puts it up on the Christmas tree.)*

STARMAN. You can have that for Christmas.

CONTESSA. Thank you. *(Genuinely surprised.)* What's this mean? *(Indicating the coat of arms.)*

STARMAN *(explains the flag's symbols).* California. Cars, train, orange tree. Double-headed eagle. When Phillip the Handsome wed Joan the Mad, she brought Spain and Sicily, North Africa and the Americas as her dowry. The Mayans saw the double-headed eagle carved on a stone. They scratched their heads. And I'm not leaving until they pay me for California! In 1938, all the gold of Orium Empirium was sent to California. It was insured but Roosevelt wouldn't send it back.

Two million, 500 thousand dollars. *(He laughs.)* On the streets. *(He gets sad.)* They won't give me another green card. I don't know what to do.

CONTESSA. Oh I don't see why not. I can't imagine you're the first person to ever lose a green card.

STARMAN. They don't like me. I don't like them.

CONTESSA. I'll go down with you. I'm not afraid of some clerk. It's because you're foreign. Some people are like that. *(She looks at the weather and sniffs.)* Channel 4 said no snow tonight and he's always right. It's cold though. Will you be all right tonight?

STARMAN. Yes.

CONTESSA. Going down to the bus station? *(He doesn't answer and turns away, working on another flag.)* Don't get upset. I'm just trying to make conversation.

STARMAN. Maybe the bus station, maybe the mission. I don't know.

CONTESSA. When you have a family, you get into the habit of worrying about people. God, I've taken care of plenty of husbands and children in my time. Not to mention in-laws. Cooked and cleaned, bathed and dressed them. We had a house in the mountains, me and the Count. It was miserable—a wood stove, no running water. I had a bad fall down those outside steps, smashed one of my veins. The doctor was worried when it got infected. I was drinking a lot I know but I couldn't stand the memories.

STARMAN. You came here with nothing, and now you have your own place. You are very strong in your heart.

CONTESSA. That's how it is. His family said I took advantage. *(She snorts.)* Pfft! I didn't like Brooklyn and I wasn't going to stay there. After the Count died, I packed my things and... I've got to go. *(She imagines someone breaking into her house.)* They're... someone's coming! *(She jumps up flustered.)*

STARMAN. Shhh, shhh *(Soothing her in a familiar way.)* No one's there, it's all right, all right. Go on. They behaved very badly to you.

CONTESSA *(disoriented, sits down again).* Umm.

STARMAN. Your brother-in-law... in Brooklyn...

CONTESSA. Don't make me stay a long time, please. *(She draws out a small bottle and takes a drink. She offers it to STARMAN, who takes the bottle but doesn't drink, as she continues.)* His brother was a twerp, worse, he was a lazy, son-of-a-bitch! I was supposed to wait on them hand and foot, *hand and foot.* And I did. I did exactly as I was told, I'm no fool. As soon as I put away enough household money, and it wasn't easy, a nickel here a dime there, I reused everything...

STARMAN *(laughs).* Yes.

CONTESSA *(laughs too).* I snitched stockings from his sisters and I smoked the old man's cigar butts! When I had the money for a train down here, I packed my things in a K-Mart shopping bag and told them I was going to the Yonkers Amvets and that was it! I had an old friend in Arlington, oh, from years back. I stayed with her.

STARMAN. Someone took you in.

CONTESSA. Yes, and I got this place I have now. It's just as well. Her daughter shipped her off to the Baptist home in Richmond and she died six months later. She was happy as can be in that house and so what if you leave the lights on. Her daughter was a tightwad, wouldn't pay for me to live in, and she died because it broke her heart to leave that house. Have another sandwich. *(He takes a third sandwich.)*

STARMAN. Christopher Columbus was born in New York in 1840. He went to Italy and they put him in jail and then he went to Spain. Then he came to Virginia.

CONTESSA. Hmm, I hadn't heard that. I really ought to go, Starman.

STARMAN *(paces back and forth, agitated)*. People sit on my bench like they own it. They think they're superior. *(He laughs.)* Stockbrokers and secret police! I was going back to Galicia, not last year, the other year, with a group, but I speak the language. I want to stay with my family, I'm not a tourist.

CONTESSA. You're an artist.

STARMAN. No, I'm not, I'm an architect, plumber, steamfitter, union in Detroit, Michigan. I'm a brother. I'm a son. You have a good time and see your friend. You're not a tourist, don't worry.

CONTESSA. Well, you certainly have talent. *(She takes back the flask and drinks.)* Does your sister ever write you? *(STARMAN just looks sad as a response.)* I guess you'll have to go in tonight.

STARMAN. I'm staying here.

CONTESSA. They're going to round you all up and take you to the shelters tonight, on account of it being so cold. I heard it on the radio.

STARMAN. No.
CONTESSA. Don't be ridiculous. You'll be frozen hard as a rock if you stay out tonight. And what's wrong with your head? You shouldn't be out here if you got hit in the head. Come on, I can't sit here any longer. You go to the shelter. I'll walk you down as far as 14th Street. *(She gets up.)* Come on. *(STARMAN ignores her.)* They'll take you away tonight, I'm telling you, I heard it on the news. It's not good for them when one of you freezes up out here. You will go in somewhere, won't you? *(He doesn't answer.)* Well, all right, I'm off. Wish me luck. Good night.
STARMAN. Good luck...
STARMAN & CONTESSA *(together, like it's an old joke)*. And good riddance!
CONTESSA *(chuckles as she leaves the stage)*. See you tomorrow.
STARMAN. Contessa?
CONTESSA. What?
STARMAN. Come here. *(He beckons her back. She walks toward him.)*
CONTESSA. What do you want?
STARMAN. Even though you don't trust me, I trust you. I like you—you're special. *(He touches her tail, she pulls it away.)*
CONTESSA. Knock it off.
STARMAN. I want to ask you...no, don't look at me like that! You don't even know yet.
CONTESSA. I can guess and the answer is no.

STARMAN. I haven't even asked you. You take a lot for granted. I haven't even whispered it yet.

CONTESSA. Well? Is it some big secret?

STARMAN. Yes. Maybe I'll never ask you.

CONTESSA. Oh, for God's sake, stop beating around the bush. You want some money, say so! *(STARMAN just smiles.)* You're a bum. Here. *(She gives him a couple of dollars. He doesn't even look at it.)* Well, don't take it, I don't care. Stop staring!

STARMAN. You're pretty.

CONTESSA. Go ahead and make a fool of yourself. It's good entertainment. Get down on your knees and ask for my hand, go on.

STARMAN. That's not what I want to ask you. But it's close. *(He whispers.)*

CONTESSA. No!

STARMAN. I'll sleep in the hall.

CONTESSA. Forget it! You think because I bring you a sandwich every once in a while you're entitled to move in with me? *(Arrogantly, with a swish of her tail.)* When I want company, I'll invite you. *(Suspiciously.)* You're just waiting for me to slip, so you can steal all my stuff. You probably want to rape me, don't you? Well, I'm a dried-up old woman, so don't bother! *(CONTESSA exits.)*

STARMAN. You don't think of anyone but yourself! Only yourself!!

(The lights of the afternoon come down and the Christmas tree lights come up. Wearily, STARMAN takes his

bags and stows them amid the creche figures and the straw. He sits with his head in his hands. The reflection of flashing red lights and sirens offstage breaks the mood. STARMAN hides under the tree. Crackled voices on a police radio and the swing of a flashlight beam suggest an officer looking for street people. After a while, the flashing lights and sirens fade. STARMAN emerges from the creche and wraps himself in a blanket. He paces, because it's too cold to sleep, and mumbles to himself. When he hears someone coming, he hides behind the tree. CONTESSA reenters.)

CONTESSA *(whispers).* Starman?

STARMAN *(in a low voice).* I'm over here. Change your mind?

CONTESSA. I brought you some soup. It's chicken noodle. *(She takes out a jar covered in aluminum foil and puts it on the bench.)*

STARMAN. I'm not hungry. *(He sits on the bench and wraps the blanket tighter around himself.)*

CONTESSA. God, the cops are all up and down 14th Street. It's not safe to be out. *(STARMAN is silent. CONTESSA goes over to the flag hanging on the Christmas tree.)* I forgot my present. *(He takes the soup.)* I brought you an aspirin, but of course you won't take it. Why are men so goddamned proud?

STARMAN. I'm not feeling good. *(Pause.)* Where did I go when I was fourteen?

CONTESSA. Galicia.

STARMAN. No!

CONTESSA. England?

STARMAN. No. Austria. I wanted to go back to Galicia but the war was on and they said I was a refugee. I was cold in Austria. There's no use to argue with your bones. I stayed there eight months and *then* I went to England... Southampton... I went to Nottingham.

CONTESSA. To the Oldest Inn in the World.

STARMAN. Yes! I lived with the widow on Mulberry Road, Sherwood. She taught me how to play the piano. I stayed there for almost eight years until I got my plumber's license. The war, 1922-1934, you remember, Franz Josef? Wait. *(STARMAN gets his bundle and pulls out a flag and a map elaborately annotated with his travels.)* Barrier Island. See? Canada Arctica. It's cold there. *(He points.)* From here to here. I worked here for Dow Chemical Company, then I went there. Shell Oil.

CONTESSA. Oh yes.

STARMAN. Over here, a smelting mill—BP. Sometimes construction, sometimes steamfitter. There is one month of summer at Barrier Island. The temperature is maybe fifty degrees and by October, it's twenty below.

CONTESSA. I guess you got used to the cold.

STARMAN. No! *(He laughs.)* Then, my papers weren't recognized in Canada, my license from England, so I had to get another license from the National Employment Board. When there was no work, they paid me fifty dollars a week for nine months. Then from there to the Ford Motor Company. I worked one job at Ford for five days a week and another one as maintenance for two days.

CONTESSA. You worked hard.

STARMAN. I sent packages to my mother and my sister. Head scarves, dresses, shoes. It's not paradise there. It's difficult to go back, because it's in Russia now, but I speak Russian. Here, this is my name. *(He shows her another flag with Russian characters drawn on it.)*

CONTESSA. Are you Jewish?

STARMAN. No.

CONTESSA. Did you have Christmas there?

STARMAN. Of course. It's not the moon. *(CONTESSA starts to hum "Silent Night." He drinks some soup. While she hums, a siren is heard twice. She pauses each time, they look at each other, thinking about the menace of it. She picks it up again each time the siren passes. STARMAN interrupts her about halfway through.)* You're beautiful.

CONTESSA. I'm not as young as I used to be.

STARMAN. Who is? *(He laughs.)*

CONTESSA *(hurt)*. Oh, it's not so easy, Prince Capricorn! Go ahead and laugh like the ones next door. She's a slutty thing. They've got a nice baby but he's foreign and it's going to be hard for them. The old dog who does the halls—never there when you need him—when someone piddles in the lobby he'd laugh his head off to see us together. People aren't kind. It's all I can do to hold myself together. I'm sorry.

STARMAN. You're ashamed of me.

CONTESSA. No, I'm not! Everything in my house is from the dump!
STARMAN. I'm from the dump too! I'm a foreign sack of bones.
CONTESSA. I'm a mangy old fox with beans for brains.
STARMAN. I'm an old goat with a hole in my head.
CONTESSA. I'm a bird feeder who's burned her bridges.
STARMAN. I've always been proud...
CONTESSA. I made my bed...
STARMAN. I've got nowhere to go...
CONTESSA. I did it all for love... *(They look at each other, surprised.)* All gone but me and pidgies. It starts out slow enough, then it goes faster—husbands, children, then it slows down again, and you don't have so much to do, and then it's over.
STARMAN *(starts drawing another flag)*. In 1917, the war and the winter killed 300 thousand people, that was before I was born. California, Brazil, Argentina, all are ours. Papalona orium. They took over our country. England is ours. There are no Frenchmen.
CONTESSA. Oh, for Christ's sake, stop that!
STARMAN. Aryan, orium empire.
CONTESSA *(sighs)*. Hey, I've got an idea. How about a cup of coffee at People's, my treat? *(He ignores her.)* Come on, my feet are like blocks of ice. It's all very well for you with new boots, look at these old mops... I'm *cold*, Starman. Can't we go in somewhere and talk? Look, take this. *(She tries to give him a couple of dollars but he ignores her.)*

STARMAN. I have a traveler's check. I have nothing more to say... Good night. *(He pulls the blanket over his head, even though he remains sitting on the bench.)*

CONTESSA. Well, I'm going in. Hope I don't get hacked to death on the way home. *(She takes a drink.)* A good friend used to walk me halfway, but you know how it is. People are not dependable these days. When no one talks to you or writes to you, you become invisible. That's why I'm glad someone wrote to me. Maybe I will go to Florida! *(She waits for a reaction, but STARMAN doesn't move. This makes her angry.)* People know who I am. I've left my mark. I have a name, and an address, and a place of birth that people can go to *and find on a map!* It's not made up, and it's the same place it was when I lived there, just about. When I walk down the street, I say hello to people, and they say hello back. They don't know me but I look them in the eye and I say, hello, dammit! *(Pause.)* All right, Starman. Wish me luck... *(No answer. She takes the California flag off the Christmas tree and begins to exit. When she is one pace short of being gone, STARMAN stands up and speaks.)*

STARMAN *(pulls the blanket down from over his head).* My name is Prince Stefan Roschelyevitch. I'm from Lemburg, Galicia. I'm clean and I can pay for my food. I don't steal—anything! Please, Contessa. I've got no one.

CONTESSA *(undecided).* You're taking advantage of me...

STARMAN. No advantage.

CONTESSA *(moves back onstage closer to the bench)*. It's very small... you can't touch anything... not if I don't say so first... And you have to stay out of the refrigerator. I know you and food.
STARMAN. All right.
CONTESSA. You can't do anything unless I say so!
STARMAN. All right.
CONTESSA. Don't touch the television! *(He nods in assent.)* And leave that thing here! *(Indicating his blanket.)*
STARMAN. Okay. *(He reaches out and squeezes her arm, she pulls away, but not completely. STARMAN gets his bundles from within the creche. CONTESSA takes a drink. He emerges.)* You're a beautiful fox!
CONTESSA. Flattery will get you nowhere!
STARMAN *(laughs)*. I know.
CONTESSA. Got your hat?
STARMAN. Yes.
CONTESSA. Got your bag?
STARMAN. Yes.
CONTESSA. Got your wits?
STARMAN *(smiles at an old joke)*. No.
CONTESSA *(takes one of his bags)*. Good night, Mary and Joseph, see you tomorrow. *(They exit together. The lights dim, including the tree lights, until all that's left is a blue star at the top of the tree.)*

END

GOLDEN ARCHES
by
Earl Reimer

CHARACTERS

JOAN: A waitress at the restaurant.

ALBERT: Easygoing, friendly, has limited vision because of cataracts. In his 70s.

DAISY: Albert's wife. Rather irascible and sharp-tongued, impatient. In her 70s.

MABEL: A kindly widow, a friend of Albert and Daisy. In her 70s.

PLACE: The interior of a fast-food restaurant.

TIME: The present.

GOLDEN ARCHES

AT RISE: *ALBERT and DAISY PHILBIN enter. ALBERT is just ahead of DAISY, who has several newspapers under her arm.*

ALBERT. Is this one all right today? *(Pointing to a booth or table.)*
DAISY. Why didn't you get our regular booth?
ALBERT. Someone's already sitting in it.
DAISY. Hmpff!! They have their nerve!
ALBERT. So, is this one OK?
DAISY. It gets too hot if the sun comes out.
ALBERT. Well, there's an empty one on the other side.
DAISY. That's the one with the jiggly seat. Can't you remember anything? I didn't come here to sit on a teeter-totter.
ALBERT. Well, I could sit on the side with the jiggly seat.
DAISY. Do you think I want to look at you bouncing up and down and grinning like an idiot everytime someone sits in the next booth?
ALBERT. Well, I just thought that....
DAISY. You shouldn't think, Albert. For some it's dangerous, but in your case it could be fatal.
ALBERT. But I...
DAISY. This booth will be fine. Don't make a spectacle of yourself. *(She sits down.)*

ALBERT. I'll go order, then. You wanted coffee, eggs, and an English muffin, right?

DAISY. I told you what I wanted in the car. *(She starts looking at the newspaper.)*

ALBERT. All right. *(He starts to leave.)*

DAISY. And see if you can get me the rest of the *Chronicle*.

ALBERT. But don't you have....

DAISY. Someone took the inside half, Albert. I wouldn't ask for it if it was here.

ALBERT. All right.

(He leaves to order. DAISY reads the paper for a bit. Then JOAN comes by with a pot of coffee.)

JOAN. And how are you today, Mrs. Philbin?

DAISY. I'm all right.

JOAN. Well, good. I was going to offer you some more coffee, but I guess I can't offer you *more* if you haven't had any at all yet, can I? Is your husband getting some for you?

DAISY. He is, if he ever gets back.

JOAN *(smiles)*. Well, it takes a while sometimes.

DAISY. It takes Albert a while *all* the time. Sometimes I think he's gone to Brazil for it, except that he doesn't know where Brazil is.

JOAN. Well, I'm sure he'll be back soon. Anything interesting in the news?

DAISY. Not much. We're being too friendly with the Taiweenies.

JOAN. Oh? And how is that?

DAISY. How? Don't you know? Every year the United States spends thousands and thousands of dollars to transport, house, and feed hundreds of them Tai-weenies during the baseball championship.

JOAN. Oh, you mean the Little League World Series, don't you? Yes, they're very good.

DAISY. Hmpff!! Well, they should be.

JOAN. Why is that?

DAISY. Well, they're a lot older than our boys.

JOAN. Really? I thought the boys all had to be twelve or under.

DAISY. Hah! Don't fool yourself. All those Tai-weenies are at least twenty-five years old.

JOAN. Oh, but Mrs. Philbin, I don't think so. Why, their regulations...

DAISY. Of course they are. They're all like pygmies. All they eat is bad rice over there. They can't grow much on that. And then, for years they always had to duck when the Communists were shooting at them from the mainland. So they didn't straighten up, you see. And so eventually, they all stayed short.

JOAN *(nods knowingly)*. I see. So you think they win because their players are older?

DAISY. Of course. Have you ever noticed how they all wear their caps down real low? It's so people can't tell how old they are.

JOAN. I gather you don't like the Taiwanese.

DAISY. Nope. They're just like the Communists, only shorter.

JOAN. Good point! Well, I'll let you finish your paper. If I see your husband along the way, I'll send him back.
DAISY. Thanks. *(DAISY goes back to her paper as JOAN exits.)*

(ALBERT comes back with a tray containing food and coffee.)

ALBERT. Well, here we are!
DAISY. What took you so long? Did the cook die, or did you tell the waitress your life story?
ALBERT. They were busy. A lot of people eat breakfast here, you know. We're not the only ones.
DAISY. Hmpff! Think you're smart, don't you? *(She helps him unload the tray.)* Where's my muffin?
ALBERT. The warmer broke down, so they don't have any this morning.
DAISY. This place is getting worse every day. What's this?
ALBERT. Those are some hash browns I got for you. I thought you might like those since they don't have any muffins.
DAISY. Well, I don't. They taste like cork place mats. I can't abide them. You know that!!
ALBERT. Well, I just thought that...
DAISY. I told you not to think, Albert. It just...
ALBERT *(flaring mildly)*. All right. I'll eat them myself.
DAISY. Well, you don't have to get huffy about it. *(They read the paper in silence for a bit. ALBERT is not able to read for any length of time, however, because of his*

eyesight problem.) My. It says here that a car went through a window at Walgreen's drugstore. *(She looks up at ALBERT.)* You know where Walgreen's drugstore is, Albert?

ALBERT *(eating).* Yes, I know.

DAISY. I'll bet. *(Reads.)* It also says that she hit *six parked cars.*

ALBERT. What was that?

DAISY *(in clipped, exaggerated tones).* It also says that she hit *six—parked—cars.*

ALBERT. Oh. *(ALBERT turns back to his food, but she's not through.)*

DAISY. So let that be a lesson to you, Albert. *(He looks up.)* You've gotta watch how you drive.

ALBERT. I know that.

DAISY. Well, I hope you know something. I think you ought to take that car in and have it idled.

ALBERT. Yeah. Well, it's getting better.

DAISY. I don't think you should take it to Ralph anymore. He doesn't know what he's doing.

ALBERT. Ralph's all right.

DAISY. Why don't you take it to K-Mart?

ALBERT *(looks up).* K-Mart?

DAISY *(defensively).* They've got special men there, Albert, who are really smart. A lot smarter than you think they are.

ALBERT. Yes? *(Pause.)* Well, Ralph is pretty good, too.

DAISY. I don't think Ralph knows what he's doing. He's just getting everything he can out of you, Albert.

ALBERT. Oh, I don't think...

DAISY. You're living in the now, Albert, not the past. Everybody's trying to get what they can out of everybody else.
ALBERT. Well, I know that Ralph...
DAISY. Well, you better take care of it.
ALBERT. OK! *(He goes back to eating.)*
DAISY. Of course, your problems are yours, not mine!
ALBERT *(looks up)*. All right. *(He goes back to his plate.)*
DAISY. Just do something about them, all right?
ALBERT. OK! *(Continues reading.)*
DAISY. Do you want some of this raisin bread? *(She has unwrapped some bread she has brought in her purse.)*
ALBERT. No, thanks.
DAISY. It's good.
ALBERT. I know it is.
DAISY. It won't keep too long! Have a piece.
ALBERT *(a bit annoyed)*. No, thank you. I'm not hungry for it right now.
DAISY. Hmpff. You don't know what's good. *(They read.)*
ALBERT. I think the President's doing a fine job with the economy.
DAISY *(slowly looking up, ALBERT freezes)*. He's a fool, Albert, and so is everyone who supports him. He won't stand a chance against the Communists.
ALBERT. Well, I like him. I think he's doing a good job.
DAISY. You don't know what you're talking about. Here, have some raisin bread.
ALBERT. No, I told you I didn't want any! Why do you keep asking me foolish questions?

DAISY. Because you're a foolish man!! *(They go back to the papers. DAISY finishes one section, and sorts unsuccessfully through the others ALBERT has brought.)* Where are the C and D sections?

ALBERT. I thought they were in that bunch of papers I just brought.

DAISY. Well, they're not. There's just A, B, and E here.

ALBERT. Oh. Well, all right. I'll go get the others. Give me the ones you're finished with. Maybe those young people in the booth by the counter would like to read them.

DAISY. No, they won't.

ALBERT. Sure, they will. They're college students, aren't they?

DAISY. Huhh! I think he's a Communist.

ALBERT. You think everyone's a Communist.

DAISY. And that girl is just a floozy.

ALBERT. You say that just because she's pretty.

DAISY. You just want to look at her.

ALBERT. Well, what's the matter with that? *(He chuckles.)* I may be an old man, but I paid good money for these bifocals.

DAISY. You just stay away from those two.

ALBERT *(for once, asserting himself)*. Look, Daisy, I think they're nice kids, and if I want to go over and talk to them, I will. *(He gets up and leaves.)*

DAISY. You're just an old fool!

(JOAN stops by with a coffeepot.)

JOAN. I see you got your coffee, Mrs. Philbin. Would you like a warm-up?
DAISY. Well...all right. It's a little strong this morning.
JOAN. I'm sorry. Maybe this pot is a little fresher.
DAISY. I hope so.

(JOAN fills her cup. Just then, MABEL comes in.)

MABEL. Daisy? Daisy Philbin?
DAISY *(looking up)*. Mabel? Why, it's Mabel Hammond.
JOAN. I see you two know each other.
MABEL. Yes, we're old friends. Thirty years ago we were neighbors, before we moved to Ohio.
JOAN. How nice. Would you like me to get Mr. Philbin?
MABEL. Oh, he's coming. I ran into him up by the counter. He was going through the newspapers. I had to call his name twice before he noticed me.
DAISY. That's Albert, all right.
MABEL. He said he was looking for the C and D sections. He said you wanted to read them.
DAISY. Oh, yes, I guess I did.
JOAN. Well, I'll let you two have your visit. Nice to meet you. I'm Joan.
MABEL. Well, thank you. It's nice to meet you. *(JOAN leaves. MABEL sits opposite DAISY in the booth.)* My, it's been a long time, Daisy.
DAISY. Yes, it has.
MABEL. I don't think I've seen you folks since we moved. And that was at least fifteen years ago.

DAISY. I think you're right. And what are you doing here?
MABEL. Just traveling through. I'm on one of those bus trips they have, you know. See the U.S.A. This is the third week on a four-week tour. We get home next Saturday.
DAISY. My, you're certainly a lot braver than you used to be. Did you just leave Paul at home on his own?
MABEL. Oh, I guess you didn't know, Daisy. Paul died three years ago.
DAISY. Oh, I'm sorry, Mabel. We didn't hear.
MABEL. It's all right. I didn't think you had.
DAISY. So, you're all alone now?
MABEL. Yes. It's hard sometimes, but I'm getting by. The kids are real good to me, and it's fun to take the odd trip now and then. You're looking good, Daisy.
DAISY. Well, thank you.

(ALBERT arrives.)

MABEL. Oh, here's Albert. *(She starts to get up.)*
ALBERT. No, that's all right. Just stay there. I'll slide in beside Daisy. You won't mind, will you, dear? *(He chuckles, while DAISY reluctantly moves over.)* Well, Mabel, it's so good to see you again. What a nice surprise. And how is Paul?
MABEL *(pause)*. Paul's gone, Albert. It's been three years now.
ALBERT. Oh, I'm so sorry, Mabel. He was a wonderful man.

MABEL. Yes, I know.

ALBERT. Well, it's good to see you, at least. Could you come over to the house for a while?

MABEL. Thank you, Albert, but I'm afraid that won't be possible.

DAISY. She's on a trip!

ALBERT. Oh.

MABEL. I'm on one of those tours, and this is just a ten-minute stop. Get your coffee and get back on the bus, the driver said. So, that's what I did. *(She takes a sip.)* Oh, they forgot to put sugar in.

DAISY. That figures.

ALBERT *(getting up)*. I'll get some for you.

MABEL. Oh, that's all right, Albert. I have to go in a minute anyway. I'll get some on my way out.

ALBERT. No, let me get it. You just sit here and visit with Daisy. I'll be right back. *(He exits.)*

MABEL. You know, he reminds me so much of Paul.

DAISY. He does?

MABEL. Paul was always doing things like that, too. Little things I never noticed until he was gone.

DAISY. Oh?

MABEL. Like when I used to send him to the grocery story. He'd always buy me a little package of cashews because he knew I liked them so well. It was just a little thing, but you know, I never eat a cashew anymore without thinking of him. Isn't that silly?

DAISY. Well, no, not really.

MABEL. You're a lucky woman, Daisy, to have a good man like Albert.

DAISY *(a bit flustered).* Yes, well... *(A bus horn sounds.)*
MABEL. Oh-oh, there's the horn. I guess it's time for us old-timers to get back to our seats.

(ALBERT comes back with the sugar.)

ALBERT. Here you are, Mabel.
MABEL. Thank you, Albert. Sorry I've got to run. Well, a slow walk is more like it. Anyway, nice seeing you again. And remember, if you're ever near Columbus, make sure you stop and see me.
DAISY. We will, Mabel.
ALBERT. Nice to see you again.
MABEL. Goodbye. *(She exits.)*
ALBERT. Goodbye. *(He turns back to DAISY.)* My, she looks good, doesn't she?
DAISY. She looks all right, I guess.
ALBERT. I should say. But what about Paul? Isn't that something!
DAISY. No one lives forever, Albert.
ALBERT. Well, I know, but it's still hard to believe. He was a good friend.
DAISY. But he's gone!
ALBERT. Yes, well, it's just too bad! *(He remembers about the papers.)* Oh, I don't know what happened, but I guess somebody threw away the C and D sections by mistake or simply walked off with them. I went through the whole stack, but they're just not there.
DAISY *(getting up).* Oh, that doesn't matter. It wasn't that important, anyway. We can go now. Here, carry this,

will you? *(She hands him some of the food or reading materials she brought with her. He starts out.)* Not so fast there. *(He turns. She speaks, a bit hesitantly.)* Let me take your arm.

ALBERT *(not sure he heard right)*. What was that?

DAISY *(a bit gruffly, to cover up her show of tenderness)*. I said, let me take your arm.

ALBERT *(immensely pleased)*. Oh... well, sure. *(He chuckles.)* Well, sure. It's... it's been a long time, Daisy. *(They start down the aisle. ALBERT chuckles again.)*

DAISY. Now don't get any funny ideas. *(They exit. Curtain.)*

END

THE MAGIC BANDIT
by
Mark Steven Jensen

CHARACTERS

LUCILE: A mature woman on vacation in Las Vegas. Late 60s, early 70s.

BERNICE: Lucile's best friend. On vacation with her. Same age.

PLACE: A Las Vegas casino.

TIME: Present day, late afternoon.

THE MAGIC BANDIT

AT RISE: *Casino sounds. Clink of glass, slap of money in metal trough, electronic beeps of slot machines. LUCILE and BERNICE sitting at slot machines. LUCILE is playing. BERNICE is examining her camera.*

LUCILE. C'mon, c'mon, c'mon! Dagnabit! Two bananas and a lemon. Mister Machine, is that how you let me win? Can't you be nice to me? *(LUCILE shoves some quarters into the machine.)* Let's go Megabucks! C'mon. This is it, this is the quarter. *(Stands up and spins in a circle. Sits down again.)* Good luck spinning before the big spin. *(BERNICE rolls her eyes. LUCILE pulls the arm.)*
BERNICE. Don't understand why my grandson gave me this camera. It's got so many gadgets on it.
LUCILE. C'mon, c'mon, c'mon! Ha-ha! Two strawberries and one single bar. See that, see that?
BERNICE. I see it.
LUCILE. Got my quarter back.
BERNICE. Wow.
LUCILE. This machine's hot. It has that click, click, right before it pays out. Means a jackpot's ready to practically burst.
BERNICE. Lucile.
LUCILE. I feel it.

BERNICE. Lucile. We've sat here a long time. Since two. You promised tonight we could catch those magicians and their bleached-out tigers.

LUCILE. I know, I know.

BERNICE. They might sell out their tickets. Then we'll miss them. It's our last night in Vegas.

LUCILE. Okay. We'll go. It just feels so close. Oh well. *(LUCILE cashes out her credits.)* Let me cash in my quarters and we can go up to their box office.

BERNICE. I'll be with you in a bit. I just about got this worked out.

LUCILE. What worked out?

BERNICE. This self-timer on this camera. My grandson was showing me it, I'm trying to figure out what we did. That's not right. What did he say again?

LUCILE. You'll wait here? I won't be too long.

BERNICE. Yeah, yeah, sure. I'll be here. *(LUCILE exits.)* Oh, here we go. That's what I do. Think my grandson should be a computer teacher. Even showed me how to do this. *(BERNICE puts the camera back in her purse. Long wait. BERNICE grows anxious.)* She better hurry, they'll probably be sold out. She's gotta play and play these dang machines. Don't see why these are so fun. *(She taps her fingers, looks at her watch. Gets up and stretches. BERNICE takes out a quarter and starts to put it in her machine. She looks at LUCILE's machine. She is torn.)* I won't win anything anyway. *(BERNICE puts the quarter in LUCILE's machine. Doesn't win.)* See. Stupid. Very stupid. *(Silence. Then she impulsively sticks five quarters in LUCILE's machine.)* Why am I doing this? Stop it, Bernice. *(She presses the spin button and walks away from the machine. Jackpot noise. Sounds of quarters streaming into the metal pan.)* Oh my gosh. Lucile's machine...

(Quickly she takes out her purse and starts shoving the coins inside. The coins keep coming. LUCILE enters.)

BERNICE. Lucile! Hi! I just put in a quarter and, and look!
LUCILE. Your purse isn't large enough.
BERNICE. I guess it isn't! Get me one of those cups, I'll put the rest in that. Sorry, you were so excited about it and I... *(LUCILE tersely hands BERNICE a coin cup.)*
LUCILE. From one quarter?
BERNICE. Yes. No. No.
LUCILE. How many?
BERNICE. Five.
LUCILE. Five?
BERNICE. But the second time.
LUCILE. You played my machine twice?
BERNICE. Did I? I might've, I guess I did. You knew when the jackpot was coming. *(BERNICE shoves more quarters into the cup. LUCILE gives her a tough stare.)* Lucile, I'll split it with you. Most of these quarters are, are your money. This takes some of the sting off our losings. Fills my purse and two cups.
LUCILE. I knew the jackpot was coming. I knew it.
BERNICE. I know you did! Let's see how much it is.
LUCILE. You didn't trick me off here, did you?
BERNICE. What?

The Magic Bandit 243

LUCILE. Send me off so, so you could play my machine.
BERNICE. No.
LUCILE. You sure?
BERNICE. I didn't, Lucile, don't even think I would do that, ever, to you.
LUCILE. Why'd you play it then?
BERNICE. I had extra quarters.
LUCILE. I thought you didn't have any quarters.
BERNICE. Had a few in my purse.
LUCILE. Those are your coffee quarters.
BERNICE. You took forever. I was bored.
LUCILE. There was a line.
BERNICE. If I hadn't played, neither one of us would've won. Now we both win.
LUCILE. Three hours I worked on that machine.
BERNICE. Let's see how much we got.
LUCILE. It's all money to you, isn't it?
BERNICE. What is?
LUCILE. The jackpot. It's only money.
BERNICE. It is only money!
LUCILE. Double jackpot. Must've felt unbelievable when that third double jackpot sign clicked on the payline.
BERNICE. I didn't see it. I put my money in and I walked away. Then I heard the coins dropping...
LUCILE. I have been so hoping for a jackpot.
BERNICE. We've got tomorrow, we've got all night even, if you want. Why are you shooting barbs at me? You should be glad I lucked out.
LUCILE. I should be.
BERNICE. Is this going to ruin our trip?

LUCILE. No.

BERNICE. You act like it is.

LUCILE. I...no. No.

BERNICE. You say I should have fun so bad but the second I have fun, what happens?

LUCILE. Let's go count the money.

BERNICE. Don't hold this against me, Lucile. I'm serious about this. What is it?

LUCILE. I don't know.

BERNICE. Then quit being so grumpy.

LUCILE. All right! *(Silence.)* Too many days slip by me back home and they are so quiet. Too quiet.

BERNICE. Something will happen. The magic show tonight. That'll be exciting.

LUCILE. It's, it's the routine at home. The grandkids call once in a while, quilting parties. But here we got...here.

BERNICE. Yes. We do.

LUCILE. Sure wish we could can this town's energy. Pour it in a pickle jar and seal it up. Later on we could open jars of it at home during the low moments. Every day that I live, I want there to be...just the chance that there might be a jackpot. But every day that passes takes away one more chance to win.

BERNICE. The days. That's what goes.

LUCILE. Opportunities get stolen away.

BERNICE. It's not as bad as that.

LUCILE. Yes, it is.

BERNICE. I won't believe it.

LUCILE. This was typical. Something important that I just missed.

BERNICE. I didn't mean to, to take from you. I was just waiting, I needed to keep busy.

LUCILE. At least this jackpot went to you.

BERNICE. Lucile, we won together.

LUCILE. Yeah.

BERNICE. We did. Hey. We should have a picture of the both of us. Both of us holding the jackpot.

LUCILE. No.

BERNICE. Who got me interested in playing that machine? You did. Stand over there, I'll put the camera on this slot machine. *(BERNICE pulls out her camera from her purse.)* I think I figured out the self-timer.

LUCILE. If you want...

BERNICE. Lucile, don't be so ridiculous! I could shake you up sometimes! But I won't. Hold these. *(BERNICE gives LUCILE the two cups full of money. BERNICE sets the camera on top of one of the slot machines and aims it at LUCILE.)* A little higher, I can't see it. Good, good. Much better. Never done this before... My grandson says I should press this down... I'll be right there... Is it working?

LUCILE. It's flashing.

BERNICE. Must be on. Kind've acts like it's on.

LUCILE. Hurry up, it's blinking! *(BERNICE hustles in front of the camera, next to LUCILE. They display their coins and smile. The camera blinks quickly, then flashes.)* The jackpot. Caught forever.

BERNICE. We should cash in and get those tickets. Okay, Lucile?

LUCILE. Yes.

BERNICE. We'll go back to a casino right after the show. Whatever you want.
LUCILE. Going to be a wild night. Our last night in Vegas.
BERNICE. Can't get too wild. I'm pretty good with this camera. Could record everything and blackmail you.
LUCILE. You wouldn't. *(BERNICE aims her camera at LUCILE.)* Get that thing away. *(Light moment between them. BERNICE puts away the camera.)* Let's go then.
BERNICE. Let's.
LUCILE. Two seats for the magic show! *(They exit, carrying the cups of coins like trophies. Another jackpot heard in the casino.)*

END

THE SALE
by
David Alex

CHARACTERS

MS. MULVANEY: Though bright and full of life, she is lonely. She could be any age but has certainly taught for many years without losing any of her warmth or youthful enthusiasm. We are not surprised to learn the extent of her caring.

JOSEPH PASKALL: An honest, hardworking young man of 20. Though not a particularly successful student, he has great insight and understands people. There is a sweet innocence about him that is disarming and warming. Paskall rhymes with "rascal."

PLACE: Ms. Mulvaney's home.

TIME: Anytime since the development of the algebra.

THE SALE

SCENE ONE

SETTING: *We are in the living room of Ms. Mulvaney's home. She has accumulated many gifts and other tokens of appreciation during her tenure as a teacher.*

AT RISE: *It is afternoon. MS. MULVANEY is teaching a mathematics lesson to JOSEPH. He is paying close attention. His briefcase is nearby.*

MS. MULVANEY. Therefore, "x" plus the fraction "b" over two "a" the quantity squared equals the quantity "b" squared minus four "a" "c" divided by four "a" squared. *(Beat.)* After taking the square root of each side, we see the "x" plus the fraction "b" divided by two "a" equals plus or minus the square root of the numerator over the square root of four "a" squared which we know is two "a."
JOSEPH. We do.
MS. MULVANEY. It's typical of so many things in life—the most beautiful are the simplest.
JOSEPH. The simplest.
MS. MULVANEY. It's hard to believe it's so easy, isn't it?
JOSEPH. Very hard.

MS. MULVANEY. After you add negative "b" divided by two "a" to both sides, you can add the two fractions since they already have a common denominator.

JOSEPH. ...A common denominator.

MS. MULVANEY. It brings everything together; like a family. There...now you've solved for "x."

JOSEPH. "X."

MS. MULVANEY. Yes. "X" is negative "b," plus or minus the square root of "b" squared minus four "a" "c," all over two "a." Do you understand?

JOSEPH. Sure...but what's "x"?

MS. MULVANEY. I just told you.

JOSEPH. You did?

MS. MULVANEY. "X" is negative "b," plus or minus the square root of "b" squared minus four "a" "c," all over two "a."

JOSEPH. And that's what "x" is?

MS. MULVANEY. Yes.

JOSEPH. "B" plus—

MS. MULVANEY. Negative "b."

JOSEPH. Negative "b"—and then all the rest.

MS. MULVANEY. Yes.

JOSEPH. That's "x."

MS. MULVANEY. Good.

JOSEPH. ...But what exactly is "x"?

MS. MULVANEY. ...Did you take pre-algebra?

JOSEPH. Of course, I did... What's pre-algebra?

MS. MULVANEY. It's the course you take before you take algebra.

JOSEPH. Oh, I took a lotta those.

MS. MULVANEY. Good.

JOSEPH. I think I got a "d" in them.

MS. MULVANEY. A "d"?

JOSEPH. Minus. And I don't think we got up to "x."

MS. MULVANEY. I see.

JOSEPH. ...And I think the "d" minus was a gift.

MS. MULVANEY. Gift—it was an endowment.

JOSEPH. That could be.

MS. MULVANEY. I'm sorry. I didn't mean it to sound like that. I hope I didn't offend you.

JOSEPH. Not at all. What's an endowment?

MS. MULVANEY. An endowment. An endowment is...is when you give someone a big gift—probably more than they need. They take it and print your name in big letters all over the gift.

JOSEPH. That sounds about right. Mr. Jenkins had his name on the report card right next to my "d" minus.

MS. MULVANEY. ...Who's your teacher now?

JOSEPH. Teacher?

MS. MULVANEY. Yes. The person who teaches your class now.

JOSEPH. I'm not taking any class.

MS. MULVANEY. You're not enrolled at Jefferson Community College? *(He shakes his head.)* You're not taking Review of Algebra I?

JOSEPH. I stopped taking math when they changed it to letters instead of numbers.

MS. MULVANEY. They're called variables.

JOSEPH. Sure are a lot of those.

MS. MULVANEY. You're not here for tutoring?

JOSEPH. I knew it. I figured you were some kinda teacher.

MS. MULVANEY. Oh, really.

JOSEPH. Sure. Who else would know what "x" is?

MS. MULVANEY. "X"?

JOSEPH. If you forgot about "b" plus already, imagine how fast I did.

MS. MULVANEY. Oh, the quadratic formula.

JOSEPH. Sort of comes and goes, don't it?

MS. MULVANEY. What are you doing in my home?

JOSEPH. You invited me in.

MS. MULVANEY. I am supposed to tutor a new student this afternoon. When you were at the door, I thought you were him.

JOSEPH. I'm not smart enough to be a student.

MS. MULVANEY. Don't ever say such a thing.

JOSEPH. Well, it's true.

MS. MULVANEY. No, it's not. I can tell.

JOSEPH. Oh, you can.

MS. MULVANEY. Yes. I was teaching before you were even born, and I know what I'm talking about. You're a bright young man. And very sharp too.

JOSEPH. That's nice of you to say, but I suppose I'll have to get along in life without knowing what "x" is.

MS. MULVANEY. You should want to do better than just getting along.

JOSEPH. You know what I mean.

MS. MULVANEY *(we sense her passion)*. Oh, I do. But mathematics is more than just the quadratic formula. We appreciate mathematics because it is nature's blueprint. And by understanding algebra, we are able to share and enjoy the revealed beauty and balance of the universe.

JOSEPH. Beauty and balance. I think I know just what you're talking about.

MS. MULVANEY. Good. If you just look at mathematics as— *(He takes out a large kitchen knife from his briefcase. She is startled and frightened.)*

JOSEPH. Beauty and balance.

MS. MULVANEY. Yes.

JOSEPH. And sharp too.

MS. MULVANEY. Sharp? *(With great force, JOSEPH stabs the knife into an unseen block of wood which is in his briefcase.)*

JOSEPH. Very sharp. I'm taking a stab at selling. It's a joke.

MS. MULVANEY. A joke. Of course.

JOSEPH. Get it? Taking a stab—.

MS. MULVANEY. Yes, I get it. I hope.

JOSEPH. I'm trying to make it on my own. *(He takes out a leather strap.)* Feel that. Strong, isn't it? Now watch this. *(He cuts the leather with the knife, then takes out another knife and a nail.)* This one can cut a nail. Here, I'll show you.

MS. MULVANEY. It's all right. I believe you.

JOSEPH. So what do you think?

MS. MULVANEY. They're very sharp.

JOSEPH. You ever make steak for dinner?

MS. MULVANEY. Sometimes.

JOSEPH. Well, no matter how tough you make it, this'll cut right through.

The Sale

MS. MULVANEY. I'm a very good cook.

JOSEPH. It'll work even if you forget to turn the oven on.

MS. MULVANEY. I'm not sure what kind of teachers you had in school, but I assure you I do not eat raw meat.

JOSEPH. Or maybe sometimes you forget to defrost it.

MS. MULVANEY. Do I look like the kind of person who would eat frozen meat?

JOSEPH. No, but you could still cut it with this knife.

MS. MULVANEY. But I'll never need to cut frozen meat.

JOSEPH. And I'll never need "x."

MS. MULVANEY. "X"?

JOSEPH. You know, the "b" plus "x."

MS. MULVANEY. You're right... it's a very sharp knife.

JOSEPH. I'll get the nail and show you.

MS. MULVANEY. And you, you're pretty sharp too.

JOSEPH. Hey, I'm supposed to be the salesman.

MS. MULVANEY. Forget the nail. I'll take the whole set of knives—

JOSEPH. You will? There's twelve in the set.

MS. MULVANEY. A dozen.

JOSEPH. That much I know.

MS. MULVANEY. I'll take the whole set, a dozen if...

JOSEPH. If?

MS. MULVANEY. If you'll let me teach you about "x."

JOSEPH. The whole set is only two hundred and forty-five dollars.

MS. MULVANEY. *Only* two hundred and forty-five dollars.

JOSEPH. Plus tax.

MS. MULVANEY. That's quite a bit.

JOSEPH. Think of it as an endowment. *(Extends his hand.)* My name is Joseph. Joseph Paskall. But my friends call me Joey.

MS. MULVANEY. Nice to meet you...

JOSEPH. Joey.

MS. MULVANEY. Hello, Joey. My name is Ms. Mulvaney. You can call me Ms. Mulvaney.

JOSEPH. Ms. Mulvaney.

MS. MULVANEY. Yes. *(She puts the knife down across another one to form an "x.")* Joey...what does this look like to you?

JOSEPH. Two knives.

MS. MULVANEY. Possibly.

JOSEPH. I've been carrying those all over town. I'm sure. Those are knives.

MS. MULVANEY. They form an "x."

JOSEPH. An "x"?

MS. MULVANEY. You asked me what "x" is. We'll start with this.

JOSEPH. We're going to start now?

MS. MULVANEY. We've already started.

JOSEPH. What about your new student?

MS. MULVANEY. Who?

JOSEPH. The one you thought was at the door when I came.

MS. MULVANEY *(using the knives to form another "x")*. "X" is what is called a variable; a symbol for an unknown. It represents what someone is looking for—a special beauty and balance.

JOSEPH. Beauty and balance.

The Sale

MS. MULVANEY. You are sharp. Soon you'll see that algebra is more than just common denominators. *(They work together as the lights fade.)*

END

ABOUT THE PLAYWRIGHTS...

David Alex resides in Hoffman Estates, Ill., with his wife and two children. He teaches mathematics and coaches boys track at Hoffman Estates High School. The author of numerous plays, including *Onto Infinity*, *Ends*, *The Visitors* and *Antediluvian II*, Alex's work has won awards in competitions sponsored by the Delaware Theatre Company, Drury College and the Dogwood Playwriting Competition. RIDE OF A LIFETIME received production as a winner in the Gold Coast Players (Boca Raton, Fla.) 1997 Short Play Contest. THE SALE was originally produced by API Theatre of Kalamazoo, Mich.

Claudia Allen is a playwright-in-residence at Victory Gardens Theater in Chicago. Plays of hers which have been produced on the Victory Gardens mainstage include *Hannah Free*, *Deed of Trust*, *Ripe Conditions*, *Still Waters* (Jeff Award), and THEY EVEN GOT THE RIENZI. Allen's work has been performed by many fine actors, including Julie Harris, Tyne Daly and Sharon Gless, and Studs Terkel performed THEY EVEN GOT THE RIENZI on his radio program. Her plays *Winter* and *Ripe Conditions* are available from Dramatic Publishing.

D.M. Bocaz-Larson has written detective stories, science fiction and over 30 one-act and full-length plays, including *Dr. Jekyl and Mr. Hyde*, *Baklavia*, *Flowers in the Desert*, *A Little Private Education* and *Replenish the*

Earth. A MAN AND HIS PLANT was a winner in the Stage Door Press National Playwriting Competition.

Kent R. Brown, author of PUT YOUR BEST FOOT FORWARD, is a playwright, director and dramaturg who lives in Fairfield, Conn. His plays, which include *Dancing the Box Step*, *Larry's Favorite Chocolate Cake*, *Valentines and Killer Chili*, *The View From Sunset Towers*, *A Trick of the Light* and *Welcome to Four-Way: The Town That Time Forgot*, have been produced throughout the United States and Canada and are published by Dramatic Publishing. Brown is a member of the Dramatists Guild.

Nicole J. Burton, author of THE MEMORY CLUB OF AMERICA and STARMAN, WISH ME LUCK, is an award-winning author of 17 plays produced throughout the Washington, D.C., area and along the Eastern seaboard. She co-founded Everyday Theatre, a community-based ensemble, and produced five plays based on oral history and research. She wrote *Southwest Remembered*, a one-hour documentary film about the first urban renewal project in the country that won the CINE Golden Eagle Award for Best Documentary in 1988. Other plays include *Freudian Slip* and *Deep Love* which was judged the Best Ten-minute Play at the 1990 Source Theater Festival. Burton recently completed a new full-length play with music about violent crime, *Last Call at the Marble Bar*, and a memoir of her international adoption search, *The Secret Daughter*. She lives in Riverdale, Md., with her husband, Jim Landry, and son, Miles.

John Green, author of TWILIGHT SERENADE, resides in Chicago, Ill. His musical, *Let It Play*, was first produced at Chicago's Body Politic Theatre and then moved to the 78th Street Playhouse in Manhattan. *I Have Found Home* (musical) was staged at New York's South Street Seaport. His comedy, *Hamburger Twins*, was produced by Michael Leavitt at the Body Politic and Briar Street Theatres. It has since been staged at the Creede Repertory Theatre in Colorado and in Paris at Theatre de La Main D'or. Green's comedy, *Mr. Happy*, was developed through a series of readings and workshops at Manhattan Punchline Theatre and Chicago Dramatist's Workshop, where it was originally produced.

Violet Gunter, co-author of CONCERNED CITIZENS, is a native of Illinois and graduated from Chicago's Roosevelt University. Two years later she moved to California where she worked as an escrow manager for the Federal Home Loan Bank. Later she moved to Las Vegas, Nev., where she commenced writing sketches and plays for the senior citizen audience. Several of her sketches and short plays were performed by the senior drama class at UNLV as well as at Katherine Center, a center for senior citizens. Her short play entitled *Turn About* was performed at the Las Vegas Senior Citizen Festival held at UNLV in January 1997.

L.B. Hamilton, author of A LITTLE SUPPORT, studied theatre and acting in California, attended college in Maine and earned her M.F.A. in playwriting from the University of Nevada, Las Vegas. An actress, director and educator, her original works include *Pipe Dreams*, *Ten Li'l Professors*, *Two Archetypal Womyn*, *Numb As a Hake* and *Pas de Deux*. *A Strange Growing Season* and *Running From Nineveh* enjoyed concurrent world premieres in Washington and Nevada in November 1997.

Douglas Hill, author of SEEN, received his bachelor's degree in theatre from Missouri Southern State College and his M.F.A. in playwriting from UNLV in 1998. His one-act, *Bansidhe*, was performed at Chicago's Bailiwick Theatre, and *Yankee Tango* was a winner of the Stages '95 festival in Dallas. He has worked as award coordinator for the Mildred and Albert Panowski Playwriting Competition at Northern Michigan University and as dramaturg for Playworks at University of Texas, El Paso.

Mark Steven Jensen, author of BUZZ and THE MAGIC BANDIT, is originally from a farm near Kensington, Minn. A graduate of the M.F.A. Playwriting Program at the University of Nevada, Las Vegas, Jensen collaborated on several projects with the university's Senior Adult Theatre Program—including an adaptation of *Under the Gaslight* and an oral history revue entitled *Seasons*. His full-length comedy, *The Sacrament of Meatballs*, was produced by Onstage Theatre of Pleasant Hill, Calif. This play later received a staged reading at the Utah Shakespearean Festival in August 1996. He currently works for Accolade Software of San Jose, where he is the lead scriptwriter for the company's multimedia projects.

Jenny Laird received her M.F.A. in playwriting from the University of Nevada, Las Vegas, before migrating to the Windy City where she is a resident playwright at the Chicago Dramatists Workshop. During her stay at UNLV, several of her plays were produced, including *The Dock*, *Kissing Shadows*, *Gravity*, *No Sanctuary*, GEORGIE AND SASS, and PAPER WALLS. *Kissing Shadows* and *Gravity* were both selected for the Regional American College Theatre Festival, and *Gravity* can be found in the Kennedy Center's ACTF volume of Best Student One Acts of 1996. Her play, *Ballad Hunter*, received a staged reading at the Utah Shakespearean Festival and subsequently at the Chicago Dramatists Workshop. Laird currently teaches oral history and creative dramatics for the Chicago Department of Aging and Northlight Theatre. She is a member of the Dramatists Guild.

Bob May is a native of Florida. He was a freelance actor and director until he went to the University of Nevada, Las Vegas, where he earned an M.F.A. in playwriting. Upon his graduation he obtained a job as professor of theater arts at the University of Arkansas, Little Rock, where he has been teaching since 1993. While May was directing the original production of CONCERNED CITIZENS, he assumed the role of collaborator on the rewrite of the play.

Irl Mowery, author of BOOK KEEPING, is a native Houstonian and has worked as actor, stage manager, director and producer in regional theatre, summer stock, winter stock, off-Broadway and Broadway. He managed St. Paul Opera, raised funds for Houston Ballet, and coordinated the fund-raising and planning of Houston's $70 million Wortham Theatre Center. Mowery has had articles, poems, stories and plays published and anthologized. His plays—finalists and prize-winners in regional contests—have been performed off-off-Broadway and on Theatre Row in Hollywood. He is a member of the Dramatists Guild.

Mark Plaiss has worked as a journalist for the *Chicago Tribune*, the *New York Daily News* and the *Sacramento Bee*. In 1991 he co-authored a book entitled *The Road to Indianapolis: Inside a Season of Indiana High School Basketball*. His plays include *Hacks, Beads* and *Vic Meets Sexy Sadie*; HORSESHOE BEND is Plaiss' first published play.

Erik Ramsey, author of THERE WAS A BIGNESS, GUNSLINGER MOTEL and SOME SAY FIRE, was raised in Wyoming and graduated from the University of Wyoming with a degree in literature. Since then he has supported himself as a Spanish teacher, a factory worker in Montana, and a carpenter in Wyoming and has worked the olive harvest on the island of Crete. In 1994, he received the Kennedy Center National Playwriting Award, and his play *Acetylene* was subsequently produced at the John F. Kennedy Center in Washington, D.C. He is a two-time winner of the ARTCORE Short Play Award, and received his M.F.A. in playwriting from the University of Nevada, Las Vegas, in 1997.

Earl Reimer, author of GOLDEN ARCHES, has had 19 plays published, including comedies, musicals, and chancel dramas. They include: *Ten Miles to Jericho, The Long Road Home,* the children's play *Jack, the Ark and the Aardvark,* the musical *Joseph,* and the musical melodrama *She Was Only a Garbageman's Daughter...But She Was Nothing to Be Sniffed At.* Dr. Reimer has taught and directed theatre at Bethel College in Mishawaka, Ind., since 1961. He served as president of the Indiana Theatre Association from 1993-1995, and is presently on the national board of directors of CITA (Christians in Theatre Arts).

Permission Acknowledgments

BOOK KEEPING by Irl Mowery. Copyright ©1993 by Irl Mowery. Reprinted by permission of the author. All inquiries should be directed to 1224 Fountainview Dr., Houston, TX 77057.

BUZZ by Mark Jensen. Copyright ©1994 by Mark Jensen. Reprinted by permission of the author. All inquiries should be directed to the author, c/o Marvin and Marlys Jensen, 2123 Co. Rd. 1 SW, Evansville, MN 56326.

CONCERNED CITIZENS by Violet Gunter and Bob May. Reprinted by permission of the authors. All inquiries should be directed to Violet Gunter, 6831 W. Tree Haven Ct., Las Vegas, NV 89102 or Bob May, 2621 S. Fillmore St., Little Rock, AR 72204.

CORNBREAD AND BEANS by Earl Reimer. Copyright ©1997 by Earl Reimer. Reprinted by permission of the author. All inquiries should be directed to Dr. Earl Reimer, 1701 Village Cr., Mishawaka, IN 46545.

GEORGIE AND SASS by Jenny Laird. Copyright ©1994 by Jenny Laird. Reprinted by permission of the author. All inquiries should be directed to Jenny Laird, 2253 N. Ridge #3F, Chicago, IL 60201.

GOLDEN ARCHES by Earl Reimer. Copyright ©1988 by Earl Reimer. Reprinted by permission of the author. All inquiries should be directed to Dr. Earl Reimer, 1701 Village Cr., Mishawaka, IN 46545.

GUNSLINGER MOTEL by Erik Ramsey. Copyright ©1994 by Erik Ramsey. Reprinted by permission of the author. All inquiries should be directed to Erik Ramsey, 2300 W. Ina Rd. #10307, Tucson, AZ 85741.

HORSEHOE BEND by Mark Plaiss. Copyright ©1995 by Mark Plaiss. Reprinted by permission of the author. All inquiries should be directed to Mark Plaiss, 4137 W. Andrea, La Porte, IN 46350.

A LITTLE SUPPORT by L.B. Hamilton. Copyright ©1995 by L.B. Hamilton. Reprinted by permission of the author. All inquiries should be directed to L.B. Hamilton, 4660 Koval Lane #23-D, Las Vegas, NV 89109.

THE MAGIC BANDIT by Mark Jensen. Copyright ©1994 by Mark Jensen. Reprinted by permission of the author. All inquiries should be directed to the author, c/o Marvin and Marlys Jensen, 2123 Co. Rd. 1 SW, Evansville, MN 56326.

A MAN AND HIS PLANT by D.M Bocaz-Larson. Copyright ©1990 by D.M. Bocaz-Larson. Reprinted by permission of the author. All inquiries should be directed to D.M. Bocaz-Larson, P. O. Box 423, Dubois, ID 83423.

THE MEMORY CLUB OF AMERICA by Nicole J. Burton. Copyright ©1990 by Nicole J. Burton. Reprinted by permission of the author. All inquiries should be directed to Nicole J. Burton, 4712 Oliver St., Riverdale, MD 20737.

PAPER WALLS by Jenny Laird. Copyright ©1994 by Jenny Laird. Reprinted by permission of the author. All inquiries should be directed to Jenny Laird, 2253 N. Ridge #3F, Chicago, IL 60201.

PUT YOUR BEST FOOT FORWARD by Kent R. Brown. Copyright ©1987 by Kent R. Brown. Reprinted by permission of the author. All inquiries should be directed to Kent R. Brown, 122 Stillson Rd., Fairfield, CT 06432.

RIDE OF A LIFETIME by David Alex. Copyright ©1995 by David Alex. Reprinted by permission of the author. All inquiries should be directed to David Alex, 1060 Warwick Cr. North, Hoffman Estates, IL 60194.

THE SALE by David Alex. Copyright ©1996 by David Alex. Reprinted by permission of the author. All inquiries should be directed to David Alex, 1060 Warwick Cr. North, Hoffman Estates, IL 60194.

SEEN by Douglas Hill. Copyright ©1997 by Douglas Hill. Reprinted by permission of the author. All inquiries should be directed to Douglas Hill, 2255 E. Sunset Rd. Apt. 1045, Las Vegas, NV 89119 (until 5/98). Permanent address (parents): P.O. Box 255, Cassville, MO 65625

SOME SAY FIRE by Erik Ramsey. Copyright ©1994 by Erik Ramsey. Reprinted by permission of the author. All inquiries should be directed to Erik Ramsey, 2300 W. Ina Rd. #10307, Tucson, AZ 85741.

STARMAN, WISH ME LUCK by Nicole J. Burton. Copyright ©1985 by Nicole J. Burton. Reprinted by permission of the author. All inquiries should be directed to Nicole J. Burton, 4712 Oliver St., Riverdale, MD 20737.

THERE WAS A BIGNESS by Erik Ramsey. Copyright ©1994 by Erik Ramsey. Reprinted by permission of the author. All inquiries should be directed to Erik Ramsey, 2300 W. Ina Rd. #10307, Tucson, AZ 85741.

THEY EVEN GOT THE RIENZI by Claudia Allen. Copyright ©1988 by Claudia Allen. Reprinted by permission of the author. All inquiries should be directed to Claudia Allen, 1050 W. George St. #209, Chicago, IL 60657.

TWILIGHT SERENADE by John Green. Copyright ©1995 by John Green. Reprinted by permission of the author. All inquiries should be directed to John Green, 1258 W. Hood, 2nd, Chicago, IL 60660.

"Some Say Fire"